WILD SERVICE

WILD SERVICE

Why Nature Needs You

Edited by

Nick Hayes

with

Jon Moses

BLOOMSBURY PUBLISHING
LONDON · OXFORD · NEW YORK · NEW DELHI · SYDNEY

BLOOMSBURY PUBLISHING
Bloomsbury Publishing Plc
50 Bedford Square, London, WC1B 3DP, UK
29 Earlsfort Terrace, Dublin 2, Ireland

BLOOMSBURY, BLOOMSBURY PUBLISHING and the Diana logo are
trademarks of Bloomsbury Publishing Plc

First published in Great Britain 2024

A catalogue record for this book is available from the British Library

ISBN: HB: 978-1-5266-7331-2; EBOOK: 978-1-5266-7329-9; EPDF: 978-1-5266-7328-2

2 4 6 8 10 9 7 5 3

Typeset by Newgen KnowledgeWorks Pvt. Ltd., Chennai, India
Printed and bound in Great Britain by CPI Group (UK) Ltd, Croydon CR0 4YY

MIX
Paper | Supporting
responsible forestry
FSC
www.fsc.org   FSC® C171272

To find out more about our authors and books visit www.bloomsbury.com
and sign up for our newsletters

Contents

CONTENTS

Prologue

The doors of St Mark's church in Englefield, West Berkshire, are open to all. Between the hours of 10 a.m. and 4 p.m., this small stone building stands unlocked, for locals and tourists alike to walk in, to pray, to mooch, to absorb that peculiar atmosphere that categorises places of worship. They don't need permission, they don't have to pay; they come as they like, and they benefit from the space of silent contemplation offered by the building. To many, in this village and across the world, the open door is the very foundation of the church.

Next door, just a minute's walk up the drive, is the mock-castle mansion of an inherited lord who owns at least 30,000 acres of the United Kingdom (the former government minister in charge of access to nature). This Tudor castle is the seat of his estate, and but for a few stunted footpaths that trace along some field margins, the rivers, lakes, woodland and meadows of his vast domain remain shut, at all times, to the public.

The grace of God and the meanness of man, side by side in the little village of Englefield. And it is not just the proximity of the church and the estate that courts this comparison; there are many overlaps. People come to nature as they come to church, to experience something greater than themselves, a silence and awe that allows them to reflect on themselves and their place in the world. We come to church to be by ourselves, but also to be part of a community, one that shares similar beliefs, ethics and moral codes. If we simply expand our definition of community, if we broaden it beyond all that is human to all that is alive, the same can be said of nature – we are drawn to it, we want to become a part of it.

Recently, across the nation, the legitimacy of this singular right of wealthy men to exclude the public from nature has been called into question. The Right to Roam campaign, through a variety of books and high-profile trespasses that demonstrate our thinking, has been pointing to the injustice of the public's wholesale exclusion from nature. We have drawn attention to the historical injustice of enclosure, and pointed to the demonstrable benefits of reconnecting to the natural world, highlighting the science that not only proves the benefits to our mental and physical health but also the benefits to nature induced by communities being more connected to it. We have ignited an urgent conversation, one long suppressed by English orthodoxy, of the relationship between our communities and the land.

The debate at times boils over into argument. On social media platforms, our supporters and our detractors debate the merits or harm of increasing the public's access to nature, with either side sometimes reducing their points into tabloid-style slanging matches. Outrage and indignation abound. This is no surprise. The Land Debate is, and always has been, about more than fences. It is about who belongs, and who says so. It is about identity: class, race and gender; it is about autonomy, tradition, custom, law, community. It is social and it is political and though in practice it simply comes down to a line drawn across earth, crossing that line nevertheless triggers an alarm in English hearts. It raises the blood pressure and lowers the tone. And all the while, nature suffers. Habitats decline. The sky fills with a silent void of insects.

It is a strange orthodoxy that churches stay open and stranger still that the countryside remains shut. The threat of harm is a prominent concern in both debates. Like the countryside, churches that stay open to the public are vulnerable to occasional damage, through negligence, ignorance or malice. A rare act of disregard can threaten the rights of others. But though the perpetrators are few, and the instances rare, the consequences can be serious for the church or the countryside alike. Churches are damaged more than you might think: an investigation into church-related crime by the Countryside Alliance (CA) – who, incidentally, object to a right to roam – in 2021 reported that 'Figures from 40 of the country's 45 territorial police forces reveal there were 4,169 incidents of theft, vandalism, assault or burglary across the UK in the 12 months to July this year, despite eight months of lockdown restrictions.'[1] Mo Metcalf-Fisher, a spokesperson for the CA, said: 'We cannot allow these precious places, which are often the centre of villages and towns across the country, to go unguarded and be so exposed.' The article suggests an increase in security measures, and greater funding to arm these churches with CCTV and alarms.

But there is another perspective. Two years earlier, the *Church Times* reported similar figures, prompted by the release of statistics from insurance claims on churches. 'Theft, malicious damage, and arson were among the top causes of churches making a claim on their insurance policies last year.' But their response was markedly different from that of the Countryside Alliance. The report continues: 'The initial response could be to keep your church locked and let people in only for formal worship or other organised events. Yet there is growing support for throwing the doors open for as long as possible.' Eddie Tulasiewicz, the head of communications at the National Churches Trust (NCT), the charity that helps to maintain ecclesiastical buildings, expanded on this idea: 'Keeping churches open helps to engage the local community with the building. By far the biggest asset in keeping a church safe and secure is the many eyes and ears of the local people. If a church is open and welcoming, local people will be alert to what is happening when they go past, or even pop inside to keep an eye on things.' In other words, the church's greatest asset is its congregation, the people who care.

There was a time in England when the health and wellbeing of nature was everybody's business, when 'the eyes and ears of local people' were present and active in the countryside, there to protect what was valuable to them. The enclosure of the commons (the fencing of common land and the restriction of local people from its resources) began the decline of our local natural knowledge, our embodied understanding of how to live sustainably with nature. Just as this new paradigm of exclusive ownership exploited nature, so it exploited the commoners; and just as the countryside emptied of people, so too the diversity of its flora and fauna went into freefall. The commons were the community and the land in collaboration; remove one from the equation, and the other fails.

And without our rights to be in nature, we lost our sense of our collective responsibility to it. Landowners bought themselves the title of stewardship, hanged or transported anyone who rejected their self-anointed crown, and when that became a demonstrable failure, charitable organisations stepped in to apply sticking plasters to cover up nature's gaping abscesses. For too long we have deferred responsibility for our natural world; it is time to take it back.

In May 2022, the Royal Swedish Academy of Science released a paper that measured fourteen European countries on three factors: biodiversity, wellbeing and nature connectedness. Britain came last in each one. The study, titled 'A failing relationship with nature: Nature connectedness as a key metric for a sustainable future', concluded that the results are linked – without adequate connection to nature, our population is suffering through mental and physical health decline, but also people are less likely to behave in ways that protect our environment. In other words, our health and the health of our nature are one and the same thing, and they are dependent on our connection to nature.

The book in your hands is not a practical guide to overcoming the pragmatic problems of public access to the countryside. That will come. Rather, this book delves deeper into the roots of the problem and attempts a first step towards a new culture that returns nature to the very heart of society, by restoring communities to the beating heart of the natural world. We must rebuild this culture that came intuitively to our ancestors, both in this land and others, because they were born into it, they were raised with it and they passed on their experience before they died. The truth, though, is that we will almost be starting from scratch. The chasm between our lived experience of nature and our present state spans many generations. Children do not learn to differentiate birdsong because their mothers didn't, because their grandmothers didn't. So we must look to other cultures for guidance. Each and every one of the essays that follows has drawn from the knowledge of indigenous philosophies from around the world. Many of these cultures have, despite the many attempts at suppression, kept the threads alive between their present selves and the old ways. If we listen to them, perhaps we, too, can begin to patch up our old tapestry, mend and reweave the broken strands.

With this book we begin to unearth the old pillars of our cultural relationship with nature. Kinship, reciprocity, guardianship, community, these were the vectors of our traditional relationship with nature. We look at the need for reconnection, and the imperative of recommoning, the idea that only by including communities in nature's renewal can we recreate a culture that takes its cue from nature, rather than one that simply takes from it. We take a new look at notions traditionally associated with ownership, stewardship and inheritance, through the lens of belonging: what do these concepts look like when democratised from the single mindset of the owner to the myriad interests and concerns of the community? We look at storytelling, singing and drawing as ways of weaving a new culture of belonging, and how our structures of education must be redesigned, to be more attentive to the world around us. And, of course, we consider the need for healing, both for our communities, of that unspoken open wound of our eviction from nature, and through this, healing for nature itself.

The chapters are interspersed with anecdotes of Wild Service already taking place across the UK, stories of people whose connection to nature has inspired them to take an active role in its defence. On their own, each may seem like using a thimble to bail out the flood, but it is the job of these stories to indicate a direction of change, a wider cultural shift that could really turn the tide. We need to translate individual heroism into community action.

The book also includes five meditations on the Architecture of Belonging, features of our landscape that express and celebrate a true community between people and landscape. The consensus that the public should 'leave no trace' in nature was a simplistic response to the plastic waste problem contrived in the seventies. But it is also an expression of a deep-rooted orthodoxy that has solidified through years of normalised exclusion: that people represent a threat to nature, that if we are allowed to be there, we should be invisible. *Wild Service* celebrates the presence of humans in nature and values these signs that remind us of a wider culture of connection.

So far, the Right to Roam campaign has focused on the rights we should have in nature, and with this book we consider the other side of this coin: the responsibilities we owe it. Wild Service is the name we have given to the culture of connection and care that we seek to rekindle. The concept of service is vital to this new beginning. It subverts the culture of our time, which sees nature as a resource to be exploited, and humans as masters of all they survey. Instead, it allows us to begin from a radically altered position of deference, not to the landowner or aristocrat, whose confected importance has claimed dominion over England for too long, but to the land itself. The threat to nature comes not from our people, but from our culture, an ideology which promotes the experience of nature as a resource to be extracted, with the only legitimacy required being enough money in your pocket to afford the price tag. The recreation industry is in direct lineage with the solipsistic mentality of ownership, a mass-produced version of the old aristocratic mindset that nature is the backdrop to your experience and exists to serve your needs. Wild Service is the antidote to recreation – nature is no longer part of the service industry, but we are in service to it.

Service is the foundation stone of belonging. While ownership imposes a simplistic, one-way relationship with the land, easily transferable in the passing of deeds, legal spells that confer dominion, belonging takes more work. Ownership does not require the owner to be present on the land, it does not presuppose any knowledge of the land, it does not demand acts of service; in fact, in our current legal system it allows for the wholesale destruction of nature. Belonging is the democratic antidote to despotic ownership, and it requires active engagement with the land, lived experience, knowledge and shared stories. By being attentive to the needs of a local area, by actively setting out to improve its biodiversity, we claim a moral legitimacy to be present in that landscape that runs deeper than the legal fiction of exclusive ownership.

But service also has another meaning, one that takes us back to the church and the services ministered within. A church service is a regular, ritualistic re-enactment of the values upheld by the religion. It is an act of homage to the beliefs that have brought everyone together; it strengthens the community. It reignites the creeds that form the hearth of the religion; it asks people to attend to the flame, to stoke the fire, to keep the tradition burning bright. The act of caring for nature, coupled with the practice of telling its stories and singing its songs, is an act of reverence, of devotion, a recentring of its integral importance to our society. Wild Service reintroduces the vital lost element in our peculiar English relationship with the land: the sacred.

We borrow the name of this concept from the wild service tree, a rare and overlooked member of the rose family, because it is a fitting emblem of this culture that needs to be reseeded in our soil. Once common in our hedgerows and forests, it is now either unseen, unrecognised or just plain absent from most of England. The tree was once integral to our society, its berries being used for centuries in the production of beer, a relic of which is still seen in the pubs that bear its colloquial name, the chequer tree, and even the prime minister's country retreat: Chequers. But there is something more to the tree: the shape of the leaves is unmistakably reminiscent of a human hand. By the end of this book, we hope you will join us in seeing this leaf as an evocation of the open palm of belonging, the extended handshake of community, the opposite of the gripping fist of ownership. In this physical echo of our own bodies, the leaves of the wild service tree remind us that in spite of the fences, the laws and the arguments, the divide between us and nature has been contrived. Wild Service reminds us that with each other, and with nature, we are, and always have been, one.

Reconnection

JON MOSES, MONNOW VALLEY

About 8,000 years ago, sometime in the Upper Mesolithic, two children are skipping across the bank which lines the Severn estuary. I imagine they are foraging – and perhaps they are: ferreting out cockles, mussels and other treats which have washed up on the shore. At least, that's what their parents have *told* them to do, keen to have the blighters shot of the roundhouse while the hides are tanned and the tools are tended. Still, they are skipping. I see it in the way their tiny feet flit across the alluvium with an incongruously wide gait and mischievous changes of direction. Each step compresses the surface just enough to mould a small print which, through centuries of erosion, will come to stand proud of the surrounding sand; sculpting in miniature a negative relief of time.

For these children, living their summers out on the estuarine marshes, connection to nature was a given. As a species, our faculties have been hard-wired by hundreds of thousands of years of evolution to thrive 'in nature' – a category of distinction which would have meant absolutely nothing for the vast majority of our existence. We sense and differentiate, adapt and intuit, processing the environment with a fluidity which still evades us in urban contexts.[1] We observe. And by observing, we come to understand relationships – hidden communities of dependence, communication and conflict, in which we otherwise unwittingly play a part. Nature's fractals calm us, its biomes heal us.[2] Ecological beings at root, we are capable of perceiving the health of an environment at a glance.[3] Nature restores us because it is us. It is where we evolved to be.

Yet it is no longer the place we occupy. The average adult in the UK spends around 90 per cent of their week indoors.[4] Nearly 47 per cent state they never have the time or opportunity to venture outside; while three-quarters of children spend less time outdoors than prison inmates.[5] For many adults, up to two-thirds of all waking hours are spent looking at a screen.[6] Eighty per cent never (or rarely) watch wildlife or smell wildflowers. Indeed, one study of A-level biology students found only 14 per cent could recognise more than three species of native plants. Worse: the same was true of their teachers. The UK now holds the ignominious title of the 'most nature disconnected country in Europe'[7] while a 2022 survey by the Office of National Statistics found that half of its citizens feel no sense of belonging to where they live.[8] We are becoming a lonely species, unstitched from the tapestry of life. Its consequence, in the words of Robin Wall Kimmerer, is a 'deep, unnamed sadness stemming from estrangement from the rest of creation'.[9]

The past echoes, and old layers rise to the surface in new forms. Eight thousand years after the Mesolithic children put down their footprints, and about four miles east as the crane flies, a young Jon Moses takes his own first, free steps on the boardwalks of the local nature reserve, in an area now known as the Gwent Levels. He stares out from dusty hides at the strutting waders making use of the recently rewetted marsh and, with awkward, cursive strokes, writes down what he sees. Teal and reed warbler, dragonfly and heron. Nothing *exciting* (the unspoken hope of otters clouds all other considerations) yet also quietly thrilling: the majestic ordinary, now fast becoming extraordinary.

I would not have understood what I was doing in that hide as 'nature connection' any more than my Mesolithic ancestors. Yet my experience of childhood was markedly different. Our wee ancestral foragers were skilled actors in an altered but still wild environment, taught from a young age to understand the distinctions which would be crucial to their ability to survive. While they, too, would have lily-padded their way between the raised grounds of the marsh, they did so with an agency I did not possess. Shuffling past the visitor centre and confined in the hide, I was to be understood as engaging in a Proper and Appropriate Form of Recreation. Nature was neither a matter of survival, nor was it simply life. I met it the way one meets it in a zoo, or on safari: peering out from the wooden hut as though separated by an invisible screen.

Connection is an imperative necessitated by a prefix. Somewhere in the course of those 8,000 years, the noun had entered our vocabulary like a siren. Somewhere, there had been a disconnection.

Dig where you stand and you'll find what you need. In the months after I encountered the children's footprints on the sandbank, I began to trace the tracks between their steps and my own. A passage of centuries which had seen the marshland of the Level tamed and drained, only for the wild and the water to sporadically return again. Roman legions came and went. Great floods swept the marsh. Up went a vast sea wall to keep the waters out. Down went fences and hedges to keep livestock in. A land of auroch, crane, wader and wolf became one of ditch and reen, cattle and crop.

By the end of the eighteenth century, this patchwork landscape had found an uneasy balance. The marsh, like many
other wetlands around Britain, had been subject to improvised
enclosures long before other parts of the country, as invading
armies and enterprising monks sought to exploit the fertility of
the soils at the expense of the wild fecundity of the waters. But
on the Level, large sections of swampy 'moor' still remained.
These open, unfenced lands provided rights of grazing, forage
and fuel to those who did not own the land but whom custom
endowed with the authority to use and manage. At their height,
such commons and 'wastes' covered as much as half of Britain
and a third of England, providing a baseline of security to much
of its rural peasantry – as well as space to roam, play and cause
mischief. Now, though, a particular class of gentleman had them
in his sights.

Enter Charles Hassall: surveyor and militiaman, sometime
duellist and agrarian lobbyist. Of people, Hassall didn't think
much. Of nature, even less. Part of a wave of agricultural
'improvers', whose arguments predominated between the
mid-eighteenth and nineteenth centuries, Hassall was tasked
with writing a great survey of the county of Monmouthshire –
one of many produced across the country to marshal the case
for enclosure.* And he did not like what he could see. In the
view of such men, the uncultivated ground of the commons,
moors and wastes was a hellish inefficiency. Valuable crop-
land was right there for the taking, remaining 'at present in

---

*The project was pioneered by John Sinclair, a member of the Scottish aristoc-
racy who played his own part in the Clearances, replacing existing tenants with his
favourite breed of Cheviot sheep. Like many men of his kind, Sinclair was also a
major slave owner, profiting from the exploitation of more than 600 slaves at his
plantation in St Vincent.

a state of nature'.[10] One just had to find the means to get the commoners off it.

Unsurprisingly, the commoners had other ideas.

'A most ridiculous prejudice influences the minds of some of the inhabitants of the level,' Hassall sniffed, in his 1815 survey. Just like their countrymen in the uplands, the marshland commoners

> cannot discern any proposed improvement without feeling alarmed for its consequences and concluding that it is meant to undo all that they have been in the habit of considering as essential to their welfare.

But what did Hassall mean by 'improvement'? And why were the inhabitants of the Levels so suspicious of its prescriptions? Hassall's own recording of the commoners' objections, despite the low merit he assigned them, give us some indication:

> The supposed advantages derived by cottagers, in having food for a few sheep and geese on a neighbouring common, have usually been brought forward as objections to the inclosing system ... If it could even be proved, that some cottagers were deprived of a few trifling advantages, yet the small losses of individuals ought not to stand in the way of certain improvements on a large scale. Besides, the augmentation in demand for the cottager's labour, will much overpay his loss by this trifling privation.[11]

The pact the improvers were offering was clear: give up your right to waste and common and the 'trifling advantages' they bestowed. Let the land be fenced and drained, and exclusive

dominion be given to those who owned it – or could afford it.* Then, everybody will benefit: the labourer, because bringing common into cultivation would create fresh demand for rural labour. The landowner, because 'the lands so relieved would very soon become of double their present value', and the country at large, because 'gentlemen farmers, who may set examples of improved cultivation … break the routine of ignorance and prejudice in the conduct of farms, that had been handed down from father to son for successive ages'.[12] 'Pact', of course, implies that the commoners had much of a say.

They didn't.† Over the next fifty years, the transformation of the marsh, first begun by Roman soldiers then perpetuated by earnest abbots, was completed: the last of the moors, like large tracts of the rest of Britain, were enclosed. The levellers were shut out of the Level, with wage labour their only route back in. And, with them, the last redoubts of wetland in which the otters thrived and the bitterns boomed. Bird, beast, commoner: all became extinct.

A tiny space left for people to be 'in' nature, a tiny space 'left' for nature. A tiny place to artificially connect what has been artificially disconnected. Yet the Machine still wanted more.

A few years before that day in the hide I had attended my first ever protest against the M4 relief road which was scheduled to smash its way past the nature reserve. While the children of Goldcliff sands left us their footprints, somewhere in the archive

---

*In this case, Eton College, Britain's most (in)famous private school, which has reliably served as a conveyor belt ushering the ruling class into power ever since.
†Though a range of strategies were deployed across the country at different periods to demonstrate consent, from buying off the larger freeholders to more coercive tactics.

is my own contribution to the historical record: doleful eyes staring at a TV anchor enquiring why I didn't want a motorway smashed through my wetland. Aged four, I had few answers – I have more now.

The proposal hung over the Levels for decades like a low estuarine mist, finding advocates in both major parties and hostility from anyone who lived nearby. A campaign to Save the Gwent Levels was spearheaded by the Wildlife Trust. Petitions with tens of thousands of names. Legal interventions. Reports. Studies. All boosted, supported, funded by diligent activists forsaking Saturday evenings and Sunday mornings. Or stealing away the dawn hours on workdays to get a gentle thing done and keep a vulnerable thing alive. These are the 'eco-zealots', the signed-up members of the 'anti-growth coalition', the green fanatics and wildlife warriors routinely derided by governments and the tabloid press. They mostly consist of people like Gill, the middle-aged lady round the corner who happens to really like butterflies.

Since its enclosure, access to the Levels had become piecemeal and fragmentary. While ascribing a consciousness of a 'right to roam' on the commons would be anachronistic – such concepts emerged in hindsight as the once-commoners sought a language to contest their loss – the reality of the enclosure's geography was an increasingly impermeable landscape. Today, the nature reserve is not much bigger than a thumb print on the map, the footpath little more than a dribble along a hardcore track. Yet even this was just enough to still make the Level valued. Resistance to the road grew fiercer and, in 2019, the newly elected first minister cancelled the scheme. It was the first time in my life a politician had watched the Machine grinding towards them and, rather than jumping in the cab to stick their foot on the accelerator, switched off the ignition instead.

It's hard for us today to think of the land in the terms of the commoners who once lived it. The historian J. M. Neeson describes it as a form of 'possession without ownership', a model of rural life directed neither by the Improver's zeal for profit, nor the Lord's demand for subordination. Commoners simply lived. And living was enough. In Neeson's terms they 'had little but also wanted less'. Valuing freedom over accumulation, commoners were 'poor but not paupers', drawing sufficient nourishment from the land to confer some autonomy over how they spent their time and to whom they owed it.[13]

But this attitude represented an obstacle to the landed interest. It kept wages high, because commoners were broadly free from the disciplining force of starvation. And high wages for task work meant shorter working days: five o'clock in Devon, as early as 3.30 in Hampshire.[14] The routines of such pastoral living also left space in the calendar for parallel ways of being. In places such as the Sussex Weald, where the heavy clay soils protected the landscape from more industrial innovations in arable farming, a different kind of rural economy flourished: with handicrafts 'based on local materials such as clay, wood, bark, hides and skins, iron and cloth' attracting people from across the country.[15] By the Tudor period this converted a poor, hidden frontier into one of the wealthiest districts in England: one comparatively free from the shadow of the Big House and proprietorship of the local Lord.[16]

No such luck in Gloucestershire. In the county next door to the Levels, Hassall's fellow surveyor, the priest and antiquary Thomas Rudge, was conducting his own County report, and reaching damning conclusions about the threat represented by just such freedoms. 'The greatest of evils to agriculture would be to place the labourer in a state of independence, and thus destroy the indispensable gradations of society,' he railed in his 1807 survey, arguing that:

> the great body of mankind, being obliged to live with, and by each other, must necessarily consist of proprietors and workmen; and if it be allowed that the dependence of a regular supply of crops rests, among other things, on the regular services of the latter, it is surely an experiment not altogether without danger, to place them in such a situation as will cause them to remit a portion of their labour, at a time, perhaps, when it is most wanted.[17]

Or, as he put it more candidly in a treatise on labourers' cottages:

> It is important to determine, to what size a cottager's garden ought to be extended ... it ought not to be extended so far as to occupy too great a portion of the labourer's time: nor, however beautiful it may be in theory, to raise the lower orders to a situation of comparative independence.

Other surveyors, such as the agriculturalist Charles Vancouver (who had a particular penchant for bog drainage and deforestation) gave similar instruction. He advised that labourers were 'much better to themselves, their families, and the public at large' when moved out of the village (where they are 'grouped together in gossips') to cottages belonging to the farms where they were employed. 'On the sides of the wastes and commons', Vancouver warned, labourers 'become in a manner independent of the farmers and many of the country gentlemen' and therefore prone to creating difficulties.[18] He cautioned strongly against teaching any peasant to read or write.

Even by these low standards, the priestly Rudge delved into the minutiae of the problem with psychopathic detail. Labourers, he reasoned, had to have some means of subsistence, otherwise they might become reliant on parish relief or – God forbid – higher wages, in order to survive. But the key was to give them *just enough* means to subsist without eating up time spent waging for their proprietor.* Owning cows was out (their management was too time-consuming, such that 'the evil will overbalance the good'. Pigs were fine. But of the hedgerows and fruit trees, which might bedeck the fields of a naïve landowner, Rudge gave strong counsel:

> Medlars (mespilus germanica), might be raised in great quantities, by being engrafted on white-thorn stems; but the hedgerow is an inconvenient situation for them: it is bad policy to increase temptations to theft; the idle among the poor are already too prone to depredation, and would be still less inclined to work, if every hedge furnished the means of support.

Medlar was not the only accidental bounty to avoid. 'The hazel, indeed, by the temptation of its fruit, defeats the intention, as do some others which have been recommended, among which are chestnuts.' Apple and pear trees, while great for the burgeoning trade in cider and perry, should also, he advised, be kept well away from the hedgeline, lest 'it furnishes a temptation to theft and plunder'.[19]

For Hassall, Rudge and their fellow improvers, 'the inclosure of the wastes would increase the number of hands for labour, by removing the means of subsisting in idleness'.[20] For everyone

---

*Rudge did caveat his position with a sort of proto-Thatcherism, arguing that self-sacrificing labourers ought to be given the opportunity to 'inclose a garden, of a limited extent, from the waste' until 'by idleness and vice he should become unworthy of encouragement'.

else, the countryside was to be impoverished. Not as an unforeseen consequence of 'improvement', but as a conscious means of transforming a recalcitrant rural class living autonomously into obliging wage labourers, impelled to live dependently.

We should be careful not to overly romanticise the commons. Rural poverty could be grinding, even with the common as a fallback. And it would be dubious to read a kind of proto-environmentalism into management of the common itself. Commons were kept in balance by those who held rights to them primarily to ensure enough was left for everyone to get by: the manorial records demonstrate the many arguments which ensued when they didn't. Environmental benefits were perhaps incidental, or at least entangled with self-interest: a system of open grazing meant livestock were unlikely to overgraze one area, perhaps facilitating naturally the 'mob grazing' which progressive farmers today artificially imitate for its ecological benefits. On the commons, land was valuable for what it could naturally provide, not simply what it could be forced to produce. Enhanced biodiversity was a likely side beneficiary.

Still, other sources suggest we should not entirely discount the idea either. The 'peasant poetry' of John Clare, the Northamptonshire writer who documented the transformation of his rural parish by enclosure, is rife with themes which still resonate in an era of ecological consciousness. In his most famous poem, 'The Mores', Clare wrote how a landscape once 'Bespread with rush and one eternal green' became one where 'The greens the Meadows and the moors / Are all cut up and done' and 'scarce a greensward spot' remained. In their place ruled 'Each tyrant with his little sign / where man claims earth glows no more divine'.[21]

Clare's poetry is a window into the profound psychological rupture that enclosure inflicted on those who lived through it; something we still feel in a more inchoate sense as we confront its landscape today. But it also hints at the way something more fundamental, more *elemental*, was broken. An unspoken connection which entwines the alterity of the earth deep into the strata of our selves.

In 1818, around the same time Hassall and Rudge were writing their surveys, Clare wrote a poem about his favourite brook, Round-Oak Waters. The name was now an elegy: its bankside trees had been felled during the surrounding land's enclosure. Throughout Clare's lament we move between his 'sorrows for my stream' to the voice of the water itself:

> O then what trees my banks did crown
> What Willows flourished here
> Hard as the ax that Cut them down
> The senseless wretches were.[22]

Clare's instinct for animism arose organically from his experiences. When he speaks as the brook, it is not an affectation, but an intuitive identification with a place which had come to form him.* The water's state is inseparably his own, and when its trees were felled, part of Clare was felled with it. Clare is calling the land into his body like a kind of Northamptonshire peasant shaman – something his onomatopoeic dialect captures beautifully. In Clare's verse, 'gulsh' is the noise which describes the sound of a tree falling, while 'drowk' captures the way a

---

*It is perhaps telling that Clare hated the Linnaean system which tried to order the plant world into a neat, scientific system. Instead, he ordered his world through context and use, understanding plants in relation to their environment and their deeper, relational meaning.

bulrush's too-heavy head leans towards the floor. Crizzle: to crisp. Crump: the sound a step makes on fresh snow.

It's there in other ways, too. Whereas the nightingale of Keats' 'Ode' appears to us as though fixed in marble, Clare's is the real deal. He has us 'Creeping on hands and knees through matted thorn' and putting 'that bramble by' to reveal the secretive nest. Conscious, even then, of the risks of disturbance, he reminds us of our duty to 'leave it [the nest] as we found it' and 'let the wood-gate softly clap, for fear / The noise might drive her from her home of love'. Clare's breadth as a naturalist was as remarkable as it was unpretentious, ranging from exacting descriptors (redstart are 'firetail') to the joyously surreal (long-tailed tit is a 'bumbarrel featherpoke'). When the land and its creatures were threatened, though poor and powerless, his words became his talisman: a means to fight, a way to express his care.

Enclosure's advocates had a somewhat different attitude to nature. In their texts it appears mostly as a kind of pest, interrupting the primary task of good, clean cultivation. 'Where by long negligence a thicket has got a considerable breadth on both sides of a hedge,' wrote Hassall, 'it becomes a harbour for birds and for various insects which are very injurious to the adjacent crops of corn.'

> In all such situations, it is prudent to clear and cultivate the land to the fence ... to remove from it the mischiefs occasioned by birds and insects, and the damage done in autumn by the immense quantity of leaves shed upon the adjacent ground.[23]

The malice Rudge reserved for hedgerow-pilfering commoners was matched only by his contempt for just about every plant in the English countryside. Black knap is a 'vile and worthless weed' and, despite its value to myriad butterflies, to be 'ploughed up, and converted to a better purpose'. Docks are 'evil' – 'extremely injurious to the herbage of pasture lands' – but 'may be easily conquered'.

On and on, Improvement's death register fills. Yellow rattle 'no desirable quality ... ought to be destroyed'. Tansy, with its beautiful, button-like buds, 'an unpleasant weed, and should be eradicated'. Ragged robin finally elicits an aesthetic pang ('beautiful in appearance') but is nevertheless of 'little use' and 'can only be destroyed ... by draining the land'. Yarrow (one of our most prized medicinal herbs) is – in Rudge's experience – of no value to livestock. He advises extermination with a spade.[24]

Such edicts were delivered as frank wisdom and presented as neutral authority. But there is also something curiously zealous in Rudge's language which recalls his standing as an arch-deacon. A warped religiosity pervades his writing, in which the cornucopia of life is recast as forbidden fruit, and abundance is reframed as sin. Many of his prescriptions were agricultur-ally, not just ecologically, illiterate. Docks, for instance, break soil compaction, delivering up nutrients via their deep taproots, which are actually beneficial to the cattle grazing the pasture. Their leaves are vitamin banks for calves and heifers, their seeds a food source for wintering birds. In the early summer the plant abounds with the gorgeous, iridescent dock beetle. As well as providing food for wildlife, the beetles skeletonise the docks, keeping their spread in check.

This is the reciprocal cycle of agroecology: a web of life understood intuitively by those who pay attention. But then, as now, such instincts are arrogantly dismissed. Instead, it's the unthinking dictates of men like Rudge which predominate. Its result has been a near-permanent war on the natural world, manifest everywhere from the sterile fields of industrial agri-culture to the studiously mown lawns of England, a fetish for ecocide which confounds order with morality and desolation with prosperity.

Clare spent the last period of his life in a mental asylum, shut away from the nature he loved while the edicts of his opponents were rolled out, county by county, until little of his world was left. Yet a year after his survey was published, Hassall himself committed suicide. His brother, a fellow enclosure enthusiast, had died a few years previously; and complications involving the purchase of freshly enclosed land at Mynydd Mawr appear to have tipped him over the edge. We should resist the temptation to read haunting metaphors into the dubitable lives of the dead. But whatever pressures determined Hassall's life, it seems the work he undertook did not buttress his sadness with satisfaction. It poses the nagging, perennial question: who is really served when we destroy the world in the name of profit? Clare's elegy to Round-Oak Waters concluded with the same question.

> To lay the greens and pastures waste
> Which profited before
> Poor greedy souls – what would they have
> Beyond their plenty given?
> Will riches keep 'em from their grave?
> Or buy them rest in heaven?

As I grew older I didn't return much to the nature reserve. I feel a certain guilt about this now, but it's true. The signs were welcoming, the infrastructure accessible. The birds still flocked there with an abundance which contrasted with the dull surrounding fields. But there's something about regulated spaces which chafes against a child's heart. In my soul, I wanted to be a prince of the marshes: out hunting cockles by the shore, berrying and nutting in the woods, or collecting furze out on the common. I wanted a reserve that spilled beyond its boundaries and spread across my small, known world; to walk a path which followed the imagination, not an imagination dictated by the path.

I thought back to the footprints formed by those Mesolithic marsh children and wondered what it might take to recover something of their lives. I thought about the commoners, and what fragments of their culture might remain. And I thought about my friends, Cat and Kael.

Every week between the hours of nine and three, in a small woodland at the back of a Devonshire farm, the Stone Age is resurrected in miniature. Flints are knapped with primitive tools. Fires are nursed into life the ancient way, by bow drill. The embers are carried in small black fungus which adheres to decaying beech trees, colloquially known as King Alfred's Cake. The kindling flame coaxed by whatever fits the season – now, late summer, perhaps the downy fluff of willowherb.

The residents of this time-warped land can identify a minimum of ten medicinal plants and forage a wide range of fungi. They can land an arrow fired from a self-made bow at thirty paces and – if the law still permitted such methods of hunting – butcher, skin and tan whatever dead quarry might result. They can bake bread from seeds collected nearby and ground into flour using a smooth rock, to be cooked on a carefully constructed fire. Nearby, a human factory churns out metres of cordage, bound from nettle and rush. The protagonists of this impressive array of skills are a group of children between the ages of ten and sixteen; the cordage factory is an eleven-year-old girl.

Stone Age Club was founded during the lockdown of 2020, initially as a kind way to keep the son of a local farmhand busy. But soon the project grew. Parents caught wind of a strange new enterprise taught by a Mesolithic practitioner up in the woods. And, steadily, more and more sent their kids to find out. This was no basic playtime. When the first students wanted Kael to show them how to make a bow, it became a multi-month project taken from first principles: 'we went through when to coppice the wood,' Kael tells me, 'how to coppice it, which tree is good for coppicing and how to do it so the wood can regenerate.'

Two years later, Cat joined Kael to meet the growing demand, leaving a career in farming to teach ancient skills. 'I realised I was a hunter-gatherer trapped in a farmer's body,' she jokes, 'and that's something I really want to share with kids, because they're so often taught their culture is something they have to buy or be given. That it's not something they can just inherit and learn from the land.'

The club teaches a range of skills, but always returns to the essentials: how to identify and use plants in a sustainable way, how to make a fire (and only when it's necessary) and do it in the appropriate way, how to develop the tools and crafts to meet one's needs from the environment, and how to tune in to the land itself.

'Spaces like woodlands are really regulating,' Cat believes, 'it's random, it's organic. There's no flat hard surfaces, there's no block colours. It's just a really visually and physically relaxing space to be in: stimulating in a way that's not overwhelming. In recent times it has been called an outdoor classroom. But when I hear the term classroom I visualise four walls and a door which you don't have the option to go in and out of, and some windows that are probably closed. Whereas our "classroom" is the opposite of that.'

Play is encouraged as a means of learning rather than an instinct to be quashed. 'They might make a lightsaber out of wood, but that involves whittling and finding the right material. And maybe they want to attach some medicinal plants to it, so it's got some "magical" properties. It's just a different approach to learning.' The children are encouraged to direct their own projects when they want, with results that can be bold, and remarkable:

> One of the kids brought in a dead fox that she had found on the way to the group one morning and asked if they could tan it. Me and Kael looked at each other and were like ... "Er ... yeah – OK!" So her and the girls took out all the organs and laid them out on some stumps. We helped them work out which organs were what and what they were for. They scraped the skin. Collected the willow bark. And over six weeks they tanned the fox skin. It was very ... un-health and safety! But it was fun.

They left the remains of the fox in the woods and checked in on it each week to see how it decomposed and what other creatures relied on the carcass. 'And when the bones were completely clean we reconstructed the skeleton.' The girl took its skull home. This is not nature connection as it's sold in forest bathing brochures. It's visceral and real, exercising instincts worked deep into our species-being, reminding us, as Cat put it, that 'we are the total sum of our ancestors'.

Kael observes how certain materials they teach with seem to ignite a kind of ancestral memory, the tactile echo of relationships lapsed but not forgotten:

> Kids absolutely love flint. They love the look of it. They want to hold it. They instinctively want to use it before you even say anything. It's really quite magical to watch ... it's like "oh wow, this is part of our family – this is us". We try and give this perspective that there is not just beauty and peace in nature but a space that is timeless. It has been like that for our ancestors, more or less. And we've got a place there.

Back home, Cat has her own impressive collection of skulls. And paws. Animal hides are stretched out to dry on the washing line. Fur skins cover the bed sheets. There are jars of medicinal herbs in the pantry and handmade tools on the shelves. Even when she worked as a professional grower she was more attracted to the marginal land at the field fringe than the crops in the middle of it, valuing the hated 'weeds' more than the cultivated plants.

> It would actually break my heart to remove them in favour of the things we were trying to grow, a lot of which I couldn't even eat [she's intolerant] – and yet I was removing all these amazing nutritional, medicinal, and historically important plants to do it.

In her breaks she foraged couch grass and nettle seeds, plantain and eyebright 'and I'd come home with bags of these things, having been all day at a vegetable farm!'

Though Dartmoor, where Cat and Kael live, still theoretically has both commons and 'commoners' (about 3 per cent of such lands survive in England), they bear little resemblance to that tradition; since the 1965 Commons Registration Act 'common' rights have mostly become little more than a set of individualised rights pegged to now overpriced houses. Instead, it is land workers like Cat and Kael, stuffed in caravans behind farms or working for free as a part exchange on the rent, who are the commoners' true descendants. Their life is one of intimate living from land they neither own nor have established rights to, earning the minimum to survive while they pass on what really matters. Through their club (they're not allowed to call it a school) they are keeping alive ancestral traditions and sustaining the culture of the commons: that buried history of the countryside, which is weird and affinitive, improvised and self-sufficient. A countryside you will never see in an episode of *Downton Abbey* or hear about in *The Archers*. It will not be preserved by the National Trust. But it endures all the same.

What is the negative relief of experience? What is the cost of something lost before it is known? A ledger comprised of a thousand untaken moments, a thread unravelling the stitches of connection.

We use the word 'biodiversity' to describe the variety of life which proliferates in a given place. It brings to mind multitudes of birds and insects, or the range of flora which abound. Yet the story of the commons can help us see it slightly differently, or at least more expansively. We see how the hatred of 'weeds' went hand in hand with the hatred of commoners, who, in the floral hierarchy of England, were appositely described by their antagonists as the 'trash Weeds or Nettles, growing usually upon Dunghills, which if touch'd gently will sting, but being squeez'd hard will never hurt us'.[25] Enclosure sought not merely to stop up the fields, but to stop up other forms of life and ways of living, because just as agricultural monocultures make for ecological monocultures, so a diversity of being propagates the biodiversity of beings. Its legacies continue not just in our agriculture, but in our planning system, which inhibits low-impact development; our prejudicial laws, which prohibit nomadic ways of living and open rights of access; and our mainstream education, which separates children from learning from and through their environment, handing on their alienation.

After I met Cat and Kael, they sent me their club's handbook. In it, they set out a simple statement of intent: 'There are indigenous groups around the world who have remained gatherer-hunter cultures who have against the odds continued to survive to this day, and our hope is that if they were to meet a child in our group, they would have some skills in common to connect over.' The aim is both so modest and yet so dizzyingly ambitious that I find it intensely moving; traversing vast thresholds of geography and time in search of the gentlest possible affinity. I imagine a girl standing on a sandbank, shyly clutching a fox's skull. And towards her, the scatter of skipping footprints, pressing lightly into the sand.

THE ARCHITECTURE OF BELONGING

ROPE SWING

Just ask John Constable: there are spaces in nature that are so beautiful, they already seem like oil paintings. As with 'desire lines', paths forged organically by innumerable humans who all intrinsically feel the same way about getting from one place to another, there is a common understanding among us all of what constitutes a good spot, the right place for a picnic, a good nook for a snooze.

For this reason a rope swing is, and will always be, inevitable. Whether it's by a river, or hanging over a sheer slope of a hill, if nature and climate have conspired together to create a tree whose bow offers the perfect height for a swing, at some point in time a rope swing will appear. You will most likely never know the identity of its creator, but you will know, intrinsically, what to do – a rope swing is an invitation: come over here, enjoy the spot, stay a while. But a rope swing does more than introduce swinging to a spot – it ordains it into folk custom.

A rope swing is an example of how space becomes place. A place is an area within space that has been annexed by socially constructed meaning. Fencing off an area is a relatively modern approach to designating and designing place, but for thousands of years a place has always been marked from within, not without. Whether this origin was a feature in the landscape, a grave that honours a spirit entombed beneath it, a temple that marks an earthbound portal to the celestial, or a tree whose canopy was broad enough to accommodate a congregation, once these features of a landscape have been imbued with human significance, with rituals and taboos of their own, they *become place*. In this way, when a rope swing appears in the countryside, it creates a new destination, and visit by visit, person by person, it becomes a place of its own; not walled by private property, but rooted by popular custom.

Rope swings can become famous. On a stretch of the River Thames between Pangbourne and Goring there are several rope swings known by locals from miles around. None of them are on the legally sanctioned Thames Path, but on the other, forbidden, bank of the river. This is not rope-swinging contrariness. It is simply because the bank opposite the Thames Path has a much steeper slope, and, covered in trees, it makes for much better swinging. The one by the 'white cliffs', a chalk escarpment cut out of a steep slope, is huge. A climbing rope extends forty or fifty feet into the canopy of the trees, where its knot can only be glimpsed in winter, when the leaves have fallen away. Whoever put this one up must have been a pro, a tree surgeon, mountain leader or caver, someone bold enough to inch up the thin, wavy trunk of a forest ash, not to mention someone comfortable enough on private ground not to get the jitters and scarper before a proper job was done. On the steep slope below, someone, maybe the same person, maybe not, has pimped the take-off, building a now half-rotten podium about three feet in the air. No sooner have you wedged its branch seat under your arse than gravity takes over, sweeps you off your toes, and out over the tops of the willows that bank the river. It's terrifying. And exhilarating.

Swim, kayak or paddle-board up this stretch of the river on a sunny day, and whether it's a work day or not, you are almost guaranteed to see a wide-eyed human appearing out of the green spurge, twenty feet above the river, rushing on that mild adrenaline hit at the apex of a swing. Teenagers gather there in the summer holidays, joggers and dogwalkers pause to have a go; it has become a small local theatre of experience, where relationships play out, where memories are forged, a place that becomes important not just to individuals, but to the community as a whole. It is a place that strangers share, a hearth to an invisible, numberless community.

God knows how many seats this swing has got through, but while the person who breaks it might not always be the person who fixes it, there is a collective sense of value and responsibility to its upkeep. The rope swing is like the mop whose head and handle have been replaced so many times that it is entirely different from how it first began, and, more than just an object, it represents a lineage of interested parties, who take responsibility for it. People have experienced its value, paid out in shrieks of joy and whooshes of visceral fear; in the most organic way possible, not because they are told to, but simply because they want to, they look after it. In this way, a rope swing is a haiku for the commons.

The rope swing is an assertion of belonging. It represents a shared relationship with nature that invests its users with care and overrides the construction of ownership. Its simplicity undermines the pompous and disingenuous 'legal fictions' of property law, where swimming in a river constitutes an assault on the personhood of whoever owns it. And because a rope swing is not just a trespass, but an incitement to trespass, whoever puts up a rope swing has done the precise opposite of fence-building. Without any legal ownership, this tree-climbing John Bull has taken the initiative to erect a beacon that draws other locals in, operating not under common law, but under common lore. But in spite of how the law defines it, swinging is not an act of defiance against the people that claim sole dominion over not only the land, but the tree and the very air that they swing in. People do not swing as an act of political civil disobedience, they do not quote Thomas Paine's *The Rights of Man* while swooshing through the air, they simply use the rope swing as if it's the most natural thing in the world. Which, of course, it is.

Recommoning

NADIA SHAIKH, ISLE OF BUTE

My career in conservation started early, rescuing froglets from hungry lawnmowers and squatting over buckets in the backyard of a redbrick terrace. I saw how the water could have no life one day and be full of pulsating midge larvae the next. A five-year-old naturalist, wondering how nothing became something. Somehow, that fascination became a career.

My first conservation organisation was my own, founded in my shed at the age of seven. The open invitation to school friends went unanswered. And so I sat alone in tears, thinking about harpooned whales and polar bears drifting on sinking ice floes. For a long time not much changed. But eventually my one-person club would transition to a job managing nature reserves, and a career undertaking ecological surveys, fundraising, making tea for volunteers, writing environmental policy and patting myself on my back for saving nature while travelling hundreds of miles to see every bird species I could. I continued to cry the same tears.

The turning point was the Covid-19 lockdown, a time when people sought green spaces and the killing of George Floyd sparked uprisings across the world. Between lockdown and Black Lives Matter it was as though the reality of social inequity was being laid bare. Organisations like the one I worked for could see their whiteness staring back at them from Zoom meetings and started to crave Black and Brown bodies to join them in response. Conservation is the second least ethnically diverse sector after farming, and the sense of shame about that fact was tangible. Yet efforts to change this situation were reactive; centred on getting more people of colour in photos on websites and applying for jobs. Like data gathered to monitor the health of seabird colonies, I felt my body being observed and counted. And, perversely, this led to exploitation of the very few ethnically diverse staff that made it into the sector; performatively listening without ever making change.

Meanwhile, a strange mix of welcoming and unwelcoming was happening both to myself inside the sector, and to the public visiting nature reserves. We said that we needed more diversity, but then no one could agree on why it was important, and nobody seemed to want to understand *why* the sector is so white and middle class. Likewise, we said people need nature, but behind closed doors the word 'visitors' seemed to stick in their mouths like tree sap on fingers. Conversations were dominated by 'the masses flocking to nature reserves', like a swarm, echoing the xenophobic language aimed at migrants.

I was increasingly confused about how we could excuse such blatant disregard for people and their right to be in nature, especially their right to be in nature *and* be Brown or poor, or both. I would talk about systemic oppression and how rolling out a new 'equality, diversity and inclusion programme' wouldn't help people get the access to nature they need. I started sharing thoughts about the connectedness of social justice and ecological collapse. I suggested we needed to look at land ownership if we were going to help wildlife. And I questioned if we really needed to grow bird food in African countries so member 23,689 could see goldfinches, when we knew they could just as easily plant teasels. In other words, allowing people to mow lawns to ecological oblivion at home while at the same time using land from another country to grow food for birds. But these are not the questions big conservation organisations want to hear. I went from being called an 'inspiration' to feeling like an awkward problem.

It was during this time that I was asked a difficult question by a mentor outside the sector: 'who are you serving?' My automatic saviour mode switched on. The words 'I'm saving nature' enthusiastically poured from my lips, 'and of course eventually humans in the future will benefit.' It didn't wash: they pushed again: 'who are you serving?' They shared a passage from a book and I felt a kind of relief and excitement, like coming up for air after a lengthy snorkel. The world was the right way up again. The passage was this:

> When you help, you see life as weak; when you fix, you see
> life as broken; and when you serve, you see life as whole ...
> When we serve in this way, we understand that this person's
> suffering is also my suffering, that their joy is also my joy
> and then the impulse to serve arises naturally – our natural
> wisdom and compassion presents itself quite simply.
> — Rachel Naomi Remen

It was then that I realised I wasn't in service to nature at all, and definitely not to people. It was as though I'd been holding hundreds of little uncomfortable truths and not quite seeing how they joined up. My 'nature superhero' mask was enough for me to believe that what I was doing was whole and right, without questioning why it felt fractured and wrong.

When we see nature as something to save, as if there is a problem that must be fixed, it is as though nature itself is broken. If we look at nature as though it is powerless and needing our help, then we see it as weak. It is neither of those things. What is broken is our relationship with nature, and the link between ourselves and the millions of languages spoken by our wild kin. That is the weakness which deserves our attention. To meaningfully be in service to nature is also to be in service to ourselves.

Steadily, I became more interested in how we could make caring for nature a more relevant issue for the public, and when you start looking for patterns of social inequity *and* biodiversity decline, you can't unsee it. The uplands are a good example of this: they are often poorly managed hills of shooting and sheep. They should be damp and boggy places, rich in wildlife, with birds of prey such as the hen harrier able to live there without the risk of being poisoned. That is not the case. Rainwater flows fast on dry hills with no scrub, causing major flooding for towns nearby. I wanted to find ways to connect with people impacted by flooding and to find a way of making the forgotten hen harrier a symbol of hope which married their concerns with nature's. But unless we were asking for donations, there was no organisational capacity to work with communities in this way. So I left the sector with the aim of focusing more on people and their relationship to land, and in doing so I have been serving nature more than I ever have.

Today we have a booming charitable industrial complex, with hundreds of NGOs that have taken up the role of nature's protector. This is the mainstream model of how to approach the issue of biodiversity decline. But we're 'saving' it to death, unable to see that we're replicating the same systems that cause harm. By focusing on nature as something outside of humans, conservation bodies act as gatekeepers to reconnection. Yet throughout their existence, biodiversity has continued to decline, and our connectedness has been further eroded with each generation.

Despite this, 'nature conservation' has slipped into our consciousness as the 'right way' out of our ecological crisis. It is held as the antithesis of the exploitative activities that have extracted too much. However, the model looks all too familiar: conservation spaces have become places of business, the industry equipping itself with the same ideologies that have underpinned nature's destruction. With reserves that are highly regulated in how people can access them, often for a fee, and increasing urgency to bank more land, many are only financially viable by profiting from membership guilt and gift shops. Meanwhile, conservation has become a career, with graduates in the nature industry parachuted in from across the country to work on nature reserves. There is little space for local intuition or evolved knowledge. The result has been that we have both some of the worst biodiversity intactness in the world, and the worst levels of nature connectedness in Europe.[1,2]

The myth of saving nature in this way is maintained because ultimately we see humans as different. We are the problem. If we can just cut ourselves out of the picture with leaf-cutter bee precision, then it will be OK. We applaud indigenous cultures (who constitute less than 5 per cent of the global population while managing 80 per cent of the world's biodiversity) for how they caretake the land, and don't apply that same possibility to ourselves.[3]

And yet we still feel entitled to export our methodology of fortress conservation across the globe.

In this way, nature conservation can be understood as a modern extension of colonisation, just with a panda as its poster instead of a Union Jack. Our practice is born of a misguided understanding of wilderness as a world without humans. And as we extend this thinking across all continents, we're exporting exclusion and the extinction of culture. The recent global commitment to 'protect' 30 per cent of global land and seas for nature by 2030 is a dramatic expression of this. The West calls it a success while indigenous peoples call it 'the biggest land grab in history'.[4]

White supremacism is mirrored in the species supremacism that is central to this method. Just as we have racialised humans, with white men at the top, followed by a roll call of humans the system deems less important, so species-focused conservation selects iconic species to save while neglecting others. The system needs sexy creatures to sell the myth, reducing our ecology to signature species whose promise of survival just happens to sell memberships, too. Sorry, leafhopper, we don't need you; sorry, wren, the golden eagle got the job. In a similar fashion, the sector ranks the public into hierarchies categorised by who is worth engaging with (and whom they deem irrelevant). The whole approach rests on the idea that there are good and bad people, right and wrong nature connections, and that those who 'don't care' aren't worth the bother. If you're building a pond, you pass the test. If you're sitting in a park drinking lager you don't. Yet I've done both – they're equally rewarding.

Where Wild Service proposes reciprocity with nature and seeks to reinstate our place alongside our kin once again, fortress conservation only exacerbates the problem of separation. It is a model which is neither healing nature nor healing ourselves.[5] Like the ideology it theoretically opposes, it is also reliant on growth (if only we can raise more funds, buy more land, bring more species back from the brink, sell one more monogrammed trinket, then we've done our job: fast fashion is bad, but plush toy otters are OK). It replicates the hierarchy and paternalism of existing land injustices.

In turn, there are multiple similarities between apparent 'bad' land management and 'good' conservation. The 'bad' is big farms with agricultural practices based on always growing more at the expense of its soils, increasingly trying to maintain the same yields regardless of pressures such as climate change and recruiting pesticides and herbicides to make it happen. Likewise, many nature reserves attempt to maintain the stasis and abundance of a chosen time in history, growing landholding while excluding people at the same time. Both focus on a small number of species to churn out. Both lobby for more money from the public purse to do it.

The foundation of conservation efforts in the UK is designated sites for nature. We identified specific islands of abundance in the 1970s and called them Sites of Special Scientific Interest, and Areas of Special Scientific Interest (SSSI/ASSI) in Northern Ireland. We're grasping at a golden era of wildlife, our benchmark for how nature should be. A perfect nature polaroid. Resources have been poured into curating these living museums and maintaining them at all costs. But they are failing. Each site is designated for a list of special species, and current data shows that only around 38 per cent of SSSIs in England are in favourable condition (meaning they are favourable relative to the historical time stamp when they were designated). We have created a system where our sense of accomplishment is based on the presence of a tiny fraction of animals and plants, rather than wider ecosystem repair and resilience – and, of course, never the needs of people.

Many of these sites are buffered by intensive agriculture, with pollutants running through their heart and increasingly isolated from other green spaces, with no hope of being resilient enough to withstand climate change. It isn't working. It may be true that their existence has protected some nature from the slow march of exploitation, but it can also be true that there is a better way.

Recommoning is how we can change this. Recommoning is the idea that all humans can and should have the collective responsibility to care for nature. Recommoning involves recognising that we once knew the character and uses of every plant and the call of every bird; it is embracing the potential and hope that comes from relearning this language. It means dismantling a system of ownership where a few groups and organisations look after nature 'on behalf' of people and makes people part of protecting nature again. It could look like land being home to all nature, including humans, where we can make shelter and grow food, as well as being places that are key to nature restoration. We see glimmers of it today, with community gardening initiatives and places local people have started restoring for nature. I once worked on a project where more than 200 volunteers cared for seven Local Nature Reserves, small pockets of green spaces dotted around a town with a population of 80,000. Each site was restored and looked after by the residents that lived close by, not one of them career conservationists, just people who understood these local spaces weren't tended to and they loved them back to health. Recommoning doesn't look like segmenting the landscape into business, recreation, housing and nature. It requires re-education *about* nature *in* nature to practise reciprocity once again. It is about becoming whole.

Recommoning is a different way of looking at our collective relationship with land as we currently know it. It involves everyone in the actions required to restore nature through service. It is designing systems so that even though a person might not have 'warden' in their job title or their name in title deeds to a piece of earth, we still have agency to be a guardian and can practically do something to contribute. It is how the emotional investment of knowing the ecosystem around us can be channelled into contribution, and not simply watching from behind a fence or a bird hide.

Areas to allow nature to recover are still relevant, and ecological expertise still has a place. But it can be given *with* a recommoning mindset. In the conservation sector this could look like incorporating plans to hand over care of nature reserves to local communities, investing in education and lobbying for green jobs for local people so that place-based conservation has local knowledge and people at its heart. Recommoning means accepting that there shouldn't be a paywall to access these places; it could be letting go of strict management regimes and species targets and being flexible enough to let nature be the teacher. It looks like trusting people to visit outside of 9–5 opening hours, and making space for areas that have multiple uses – from community events to growing food. It feels like having grace for all people in their disconnection and letting go of power in order to facilitate meaningful reconnection.

A recent shift in nature conservation has been that of rewilding. A great sigh of relief for many who have criticised the intensive land management conservation, finally something which acknowledges that ecosystems breathe and stretch, they are not frozen in time and can restore themselves given space, time and a few herbivores. Yet without recommoning the rewild we will find ourselves in the same predicament: unable to protect what nobody knows, clinging to islands amid ruination, believing there is only space for humans in nature if they have the money and a long weekend to go glamping.

We need people to be intertwined with the land like brambles in the bushes. I dream of communities scattered in hidden valleys, bumping up against bittern-filled reedbeds, growing food, enjoying a beer on the grass next to a hedgerow bursting with nightingale song, feasting and conversation in a meadow incandescent with wildflowers. Recommoning will take time and it'll be rocky as we relearn and reconnect. But if clearing people from the land and making it a 'place of business' destroyed nature, untangling that mindset is surely our path out of this mess. I want to see humans live again among the full chaos of nature, healing our grief by knowing our kin once again; restoring our agency to care.

We've made it too easy to do nothing, because we can't name the grief we're feeling from species loss and disconnection, or resolve it practically by doing anything to serve. Grief is as much a part of our lives as joy and love, it is inevitable and should be felt, it will change who we are. As a culture we're a bit awkward about grieving publicly, loudly, or for a long time with our community bearing witness to this new part of ourselves. Instead, it's locked up in black and silence. We have significantly lost our non-human kin, therefore we need to process this grief together. In the absence of this practice, humans tend to jump to solutions and the urgency to make things right again. Because nature conservation work seldom involves people on a deep level, it skips the grief work. Too easily it adopts urgent and solution-focused thinking, using science alone as the default justification. If science and business is the dominant way to serve nature, then these institutions sit as a barrier to Wild Service. We are left with an unnamed and unattended grief, looking hopelessly at a world we can't serve.

Eco-anxiety has been incubated in this environment, as an unattended grief is paired with a complete lack of agency to do much about our dying landscapes and kin. Our options have largely been limited to litter picking or paying a monthly subscription to an institution to 'do the work for us' while the decline continues.

Recommoning is therefore vital for healing those wounds. When the grief is tended to, we'll start to see the land heal, too. Hold onto the central truth that we are nature, now extend that thought to how we are as much a part of the system as sand eels are to puffins, as meadow pipit nests are to the cuckoo, and fungi to trees, then perhaps we might start softening to the idea that we, too, have a meaningful place in the web of life. That perhaps we have always had a place alongside it. Humans have carefully (and with gratitude) harvested, cleared and planted, creating intentional and unintentional micro and macro habitats for life to thrive. For millennia our bodies have shaped the land just as beavers, wolves and dung beetles have. Now imagine the industries of farming and land conservation, vast expanses of land which we currently believe can only function in the complete absence of humans.

Have you ever heard a nightingale? Or just paid attention to a blackbird, and let their song move you? Have you ever experienced the rush of joy when you feel the first sense that warmer days are coming, or the depth and wholeness of knowing the healing properties of weeds? Hold onto whatever feeling you have about something in nature that changes you. Now imagine the lineage of our ancestors stretching back through time, like an impossible human conga line, ending with you at the front. Each generation feeling heart-thumping joy at swallows arriving in April, or recognising our nightingale friend back again in the thickets by our glowing homesteads after a long winter, guiding us home. All these billions of interactions which show us when to tend to the land, rooting us to the earth. Land work making space for skylarks, tending to plants and our fires, warding off predators, giving respite to other kin, too. Maybe how we collaborated with nature once before is what it needs again.

WILD SERVICE IN ACTION

ADRIAN, MARSH MAN

Speaking to Adrian is like sitting in a hedge on a hot spring day. The conversation buzzes with a swarm of anecdotes, stories flit in and out like nest-building wrens. He'll stop mid-flow, point to the sky and exclaim: 'faecal sac!' and though you missed the bird, you'll hear how great tit chicks shit in bags for their mums to deposit far from the nest, so they can't be detected by predators. Inside Adrian's hedge you have a distinct feeling of the mesh of ecologies that weave above your head, a sense that a bit of knowledge can really help you see the messy entanglement of everything that lives around us. And we're just ten minutes from Reading town centre.

Adrian has lived by marshes almost all his life. Growing up in East London, he was always out walking and fishing in the Walthamstow Wetlands, and when moving to Reading in the mid-eighties he chose his house precisely because of its proximity to the water meadows that surround the River Kennet. His knowledge of the area is historical as well as ecological. He shows me the Holybrook, a channel cut by monks almost a thousand years ago, to feed the monastery at Reading Abbey. He describes how the monks nurtured the wetlands as a living larder, an Eden brimming with edible wildfowl.

These days, Tarmac own much of the land around here. The southside has already been extensively mined for gravel and the northside, he suspects, is being kept as a nature reserve so that the company can use it to offset extraction in their other properties across the UK. He first became enmeshed in the politics of the marsh in the early nineties, when he signed a petition on his doorstep for RAGE, Reading Against Gravel Extraction.

Once the campaign had succeeded, Adrian's care for the land further deepened. One winter's day, on a walk through the marsh, he saw the mud churned up by heavy machinery belonging to the Environment Agency who had been pollarding the willows along the watercourses. They had left the willow poles in great stacks along the way, so he returned that weekend with his kids and spent several hours depositing these poles from the stacks into the churned-up earth. With the untiring energy of his kids, with several repeat visits, they upcycled the brash into a boulevard of willows. Thirty years on, these trees have grown tall enough to occlude the railway line and the square blot of the pumping station. This screen of trees gives the marsh the feel of being far from human intervention, a feeling created by cultivation.

If you look down upon the marsh from Google Maps, you will see the path that Adrian has been walking for the last four decades. Halfway down, you'll see it flanked on either side by a scrub of green bushes, which radiate out from the line like a pair of butterfly wings. This is Adrian's bird orchard. Buoyed by the parenting success of the willow expeditions, born largely out of a desire to give his wife some time alone on the weekends, he launched another escapade, this time propelled by catapults. A serial collector of wonky sticks since childhood, Adrian had branched out into making pocket-sized catapults from the forked ends of branches. His favourite wood for this process is London plane, whose branches fall to the floor already seasoned, hard enough to hold under pressure. He strips the bark off these Y-shapes, rounds off the edges and attaches an ever-expanding variety of rubber slings. These days he prefers the theraband: a tube or thong of rubber used to help build muscle in rehabilitative therapy. In the mid-nineties, he would carve these catapults with his kids, and make clay pellets for them to fire out from the path across the marsh.

The pellets are in fact seed bombs. And so that they will germinate they take some preparation. Seeds and berries need to be processed through a combination of scarification and stratification in order to grow. In nature, the pulp that surrounds a seed is ground down in a bird's crop, which has grit to enable the abrasion. When the seed then passes through the bird's digestive system, it is further softened by the acids in the stomach and then distributed far and wide through the combined mechanics of a bird's wings and anus. Adrian and his kids developed a man-made simulation of this process of scarification. They collected the seeds on their weekend walks, put them in a sieve and ran them under a tap, swirling them round with sand and vinegar. Similarly, many seeds need a cold environment to stratify, i.e. to wear down, and he simulates this by leaving them overnight in the freezer. The team then took clay from the marsh and pressed these seeds into the clay, moulding them into marble-sized pellets, which he then leaves on the radiator overnight. Not only does the clay harden enough to be fired at speed from a catapult without exploding, but when it lands it protects the seeds from being eaten by critters.

After years of this game, the evidence of its success lines the footpath. Guelder rose, hawthorn, blackthorn, cherry plum, wild rose, dogwood and buckthorn grow in dense thickets, providing the perfect habitat for the birds of the marsh. Sedge warblers, whitethroats, stonechats, thrushes, starlings, spadgers and kestrels find board and lodging in Adrian's orchard. What Adrian likes most about this game is that it mimics the haphazard chaos of nature. Just as nature abhors a vacuum, it pours scorn on a plan. His years of working for Reading Borough Council clearly inform his inclination towards chaos. He tells me: 'A lot of people in charge love management planning: in order to get something done, you have to write a plan – you have to get planning per-mission, funding, agreement of partners, landowners and the like, write down, circulate and consult your plans. The govern-ment are the epitome of this – let's plant a million trees, they say, and then nature comes along and fries the saplings with a hot summer, or drowns them in a flash flood.' As he speaks, he plucks a drifting willow seed from the air. 'What this needs to grow,' he says, 'is a fine sedimentary mud, but you don't get that so much any more, because all our rivers are canalised. Rivers need to meander, move, chart their own course, or trees like black poplars, aspen, and the like don't stand a chance.'

I ask him if he's playing God, sowing seeds. He replies that he's acting as a vector, like the birds or the wind, and leaving it up to the soil to accept or reject the seeds. 'When everything else is in steep decline, when we're losing everything so rapidly, it gives me a feeling of fighting back.'

3

Stewardship

GUY SHRUBSOLE, DEVON

Landowners, we are told, are the rightful stewards of the land. But who holds them to account? Why are the public at large not regarded as capable of stewardship of the land?

The dictionary definition of 'stewardship' is 'the careful and responsible management of something entrusted to one's care'.[1] The essence of stewardship, then, is to care for something on behalf of someone else. In the Middle Ages, a 'sty-ward' was the ward of a lord's pigsty: he looked after the swine for his master. That role evolved over time as aristocratic estates grew larger and enclosed more land. By the eighteenth century, an estate steward administering to the thousands of acres owned by a duke or earl would have been expected to carry out multiple duties: collecting rents from tenants, doing the business accounts, surveying the land. As the paperwork increased, the detachment from the land itself grew: knowing the names of each wildflower became less important than how much income was being generated from each field.

The idea of stewardship has biblical origins. In the words of the King James Bible translation of Genesis, published in 1611, God grants humanity 'dominion over the fish of the sea, and over the fowl of the air, and over the cattle, and over all the earth, and over every creeping thing that creepeth upon the

47

earth'.[2] Some environmental thinkers have seen in this injunc-
tion the root of humanity's ecological destructiveness. Historian
Lynn White, for example, blamed Christianity's anthropocentrism for causing the environmental crisis: 'no item in the physical creation had any purpose save to serve man's purposes.'[3]
But there is another interpretation, popularised in the late seventeenth century by the influential English barrister Matthew Hale.
In his essay 'The Great Audit, with the Account of the Good
Steward', published in 1679, Hale asserted that God had only
given humanity temporary stewardship over nature. 'I received
and used thy Creatures as committed to me under a Trust', he
wrote, 'and as a Steward and Accomptant [accountant] for them;
and therefore I was always careful to use them according to
those limits … with Temperance and Moderation.'[4]

Hale's view gained traction among pious landowners at the
time: stewardship of the earth was being exercised by humanity
on behalf of God, and natural resources had to be used with
care. Crucially, however, you would only be called on by God
to give an account of your stewardship in the 'Great Audit' –
the Last Judgement at the end of all time. So, fortuitously, there
would be no accountability for your actions while here on earth.

Hale's ideals of stewardship did little to restrain large landowners over the ensuing centuries. The Fens, once one of the
largest wetlands in Western Europe, were drained for profit
by seventeenth-century venture capitalists led by the Earl of
Bedford. The vast carbon stores of the English uplands and
Scottish Highlands were burned and desiccated by Victorian
aristocrats pursuing the latest fashion for driven grouse shooting.
Between 1950 and 1980, around a third of Britain's ancient
woodlands were cut down, according to Oliver Rackham, the
greatest historian of our woods.

The language of stewardship was revived in the late twentieth century by landowners and farming unions to defend

themselves against accusations of environmental destruction. In 1977, the Country Landowners Association (CLA) and National Farmers' Union (NFU) published a joint statement entitled *Caring for the Countryside*. In the words of rural policy academic Michael Winter, it 'represented the beginning of a high-profile and sustained publicity campaign to promote farmers and land-owners as the natural custodians and stewards of the country-side'.[5] This framing is now firmly entrenched in the PR spiel of both bodies. 'British landowners and farmers are among the most progressive stewards of the natural environment found anywhere in the world,' declared the President of the CLA, Mark Tufnell, in April 2022.[6] It's increasingly parroted by ministers such as then environment secretary Thérèse Coffey, who asserted in February 2023: 'I do believe our farmers are true custodians – of the natural environment, of food production, and our countryside.'[7] The upshot of all this lobbying by landowners has been to curtail regulation and focus environ-mental policy instead on 'voluntary initiatives' by landowners, together with a hefty dollop of public money in the form of farm subsidies – which, since 1991, have been called 'Countryside Stewardship' payments.

There undoubtedly are progressive farmers and landowners doing great things for nature. I've had the pleasure of working with some – from the Dartmoor tenant farmer Naomi Oakley, whose farm is ablaze with southern marsh orchids in May, to the Cornish landowner Merlin Hanbury-Tenison, who's restoring a temperate rainforest on his family farm near Bodmin Moor. Yet the beneficial impact of these pioneers remains small compared to the bulk of those pursuing business as usual. Since the NFU and CLA rebranded landowners and farmers as 'custodians of the countryside' in the 1970s, populations of farmland birds have been cut in half.[8] Once-common creatures like hedgehogs have seen a collapse in their numbers, while insect biomass is in freefall.⁹ Meanwhile, landowners have been given carte blanche to release 50 million pheasants a year into the British countryside – more than the biomass of all native birds in spring – with potentially huge ramifications for ecosystems.¹⁰ Simply relying on the self-proclaimed stewards of the land to self-regulate isn't working.

In a time of ecological crisis, who are landowners accountable to? Some landowners like to invoke future generations as the beneficiaries of their stewardship. This at least has the merit of invoking long-term thinking. But future generations, by definition, do not yet exist, so can conveniently exercise no judgement over one's actions in the present. It's the secular equivalent of landowners only being answerable to God in the Last Judgement.

Surely any meaningful duty of land stewardship should involve accountability towards the public, in the here and now. In other words, decisions about how land is used should be made more democratic. In a country where 1 per cent of the population own half of all England, such decisions are currently made by a tiny elite. There are various ways of changing that: such as by allowing more land to become owned by communities (as it is in Scotland) and by the public sector (as it is in pretty much every other country in the world); or giving environmental watchdogs like Natural England the powers and budgets they need to regulate; or legislating for a Land Use Framework to better guide decisions.

But we also need to fashion a new social contract between the landed and the landless. A contract that acknowledges land will continue to be owned, while challenging some of the 'bundle of rights' that have accrued around those concepts of ownership: the right of landowners to exclude others, and their right to destroy nature. Part of that social contract needs to be a willingness of landowners to be held accountable for what they do. And there's plenty that we, the public, can do to start scrutinising the use and abuse of land.

The first step is to start with ourselves, and recognise how disconnected we've become from the rest of the natural world. Enclosure, urbanisation, industrialisation, digitisation: the last 200 years have seen us Britons become ever more cut off from experiencing nature, often as a result of processes that we as individuals cannot control. This alienation from the rest of the natural world has impacted our mental and physical health, and it's also numbed us to the scale of ecological loss our world is experiencing. Ecologists speak about 'shifting baseline syndrome' to describe how we have forgotten the biodiversity we once had, while botanists alert us to the rise of 'plant blindness' – a myopic tendency that many of us have developed towards plants, leaving the public unable to recognise and name even common species. 'Botany, once a compulsory component of many biology degrees and school programmes, is now practically non-existent in the United Kingdom,' warns a recent scientific paper. It's estimated that for every 185 UK students of biological science, just a single student of botany is produced.[11]

But there are groups starting to push back against this loss of public ecological knowledge. In 2020, the campaigner Sophie Leguil set up an initiative named 'More Than Weeds', aiming to reclaim wildflowers from the ignominy of being branded weeds.[12] During the coronavirus lockdowns, Plymouth-based teacher Liz Richmond founded a group, Rebel Botanists, and started chalking the Latin and common names of wild plants onto the pavements where they found them growing. 'We're all just amateurs, so that's the rebellious bit,' she told the BBC – although, bizarrely, their educational service counts as graffiti, so is technically a criminal offence. Undeterred, the Rebel Botanists have continued their mission of reversing plant blindness among the public – not only through 'walk and chalk'

sessions, but also through rejuvenating neglected parks and allotments, and getting residents to protect grass verges from overzealous mowing by the city council.[13]

Re-enchanting the public with nature is only the first step in training up a new generation of 'nature's whistleblowers'. The longstanding Quaker tradition of 'bearing witness' – of seeing an injustice taking place and providing testimony of it – has inspired many non-violent environmental direct actions: think of Greenpeace bearing witness to whaling, drawing worldwide attention to the barbaric practice.[14] As ramblers, kayakers, rebel botanists and trespassing naturalists, we, too, can bear witness to the destruction of nature that takes place behind barbed wire fences, and blow the whistle on these crimes.

There are growing numbers of people who have sought to hold landowners to account in this way. In the uplands of the North of England, a network of Moorland Monitors has emerged to keep tabs on the intensively managed grouse moor estates that dominate the landscape. This grassroots community of birders, fell runners and local residents seeks to 'document wildlife crime and cruelty, evidence environmental destruction and advocate for the uplands'.[15] In recent years, it's played a particularly vital role in monitoring moorland burning. Since the Victorian age, driven grouse moor management has involved the rotational burning of heather, in order to maximise numbers of grouse for shooting. But an increasing body of evidence has shown the terrible impact that burning has on the peat that underpins the moorland: drying out the blanket bogs, releasing carbon from the soil and reducing its ability to retain water, thereby worsening flood risk downstream. This has led to the practice being more closely regulated in recent years by government.

But lobbying by wealthy grouse-shooting interests has rendered the burning regulations full of loopholes, while government-imposed austerity has left official regulators lacking the resources to patrol and enforce the laws. So groups like the Moorland Monitors have stepped into the breach, helping police grouse moor estates and blowing the whistle on those that contravene the rules. Together with volunteers from the RSPB and campaign group Wild Moors, they have helped document hundreds of cases of moorland burning – furnishing regulators with evidence to make prosecutions, and demonstrating to politicians the need to tighten up the law.[16] 'The level of ecological devastation is scandalous and would be considered outright vandalism if it were anyone other than the gamekeepers doing it,' states the Moorland Monitors website. 'It is essential that we document their routine breaches of guidance and legislation, to dispel the myth that they are responsible custodians of the moors.'[17]

Witnessing what goes on in the uplands has been much easier since the Countryside and Rights of Way Act 2000 gave us a partial right to roam over about 8 per cent of England – giving the public access to moorlands, mountains, heaths and downs. But that still leaves the vast majority of the countryside off-limits – meaning the public doesn't get to see what goes on in large swathes of it. Sometimes, however, acts of protest and transgression lead to secrets being uncovered.

The veteran access campaigner and naturalist Dave Bangs has frequently made use of evidence gathered on trespasses to help protect special habitats from harm. Dave has come to know the downs and ghylls of Sussex like the back of his hand; his love of place and intimate knowledge of the county's geology, ecology and history suffuses every conversation with him. Once, on a trespass along the River Ouse, he found an invasive species of clam had colonised the banks, and alerted the authorities – who had been unaware of its presence, despite the mortal danger it posed to the ecosystem. On another occasion, Dave discovered that a farm tenant on a council-owned farm was shooting game despite having no licence to do so. When he reported it to the council, they took action to get the gamebird pens removed. 'It took us trespassing to get the evidence,' he recounts. Sometimes, officials disapprove of Dave's methods: he recalls bitterly a county ecologist rejecting his detailed studies of chalk grassland sites because the species lists had been obtained via trespass. But at other times the tactic has resulted in huge victories, such as when a mass trespass co-organised by Dave with his group 'Landscapes of Freedom' helped save an ancient woodland from a giant Center Parcs development.

The old model of 'custodianship' – of relying on landowners and farmers alone to protect and restore nature – manifestly isn't working. There are, of course, some farmers and land-owners doing good things for nature, but there are plenty who aren't. It's time for a new approach that brings in far more of the public to help. We need to make the system as a whole more accountable, and create a more democratic decision-making process around how land is used and cared for. But the ecological crisis is too important to be left to self-regulation. We can no longer leave looking after the land just to the landowners. We, the public, have to step up to become nature's stewards and whistleblowers, its last and best line of defence.

WILD SERVICE IN ACTION

BECCA'S BUTTERFLY GARDEN

Nestled within a Warwickshire garden, ivy, garlic mustard, dandelion and buddleia all grow alongside each other. Familiar names to most, they seem like a relatively average set of plants until a pair of white wings flutter past, their ends cut by a glow of burned orange. This is not a flying visit. One of the most common in the UK, the orange-tip butterfly (*Anthocharis cardamines*) has come to lay its eggs. It has chosen a nearby garlic mustard to land on. Yet this is no stray plant wandering in from the lane. This plant has been put here intentionally. At twelve years old, Becca has spent almost half her life dedicated to the blossoming of butterflies. She tells me that each butterfly species needs specific plants to lay its eggs on and continue the next generation. Becca's garden has provided respite for thousands of individual butterflies spanning eighteen different species.

According to the British Trust for Ornithology (BTO), orange tips are becoming 'increasingly reliant' on plants like garlic mustard. However, the culture of our toxin-soaked ecosystems, forever uprooted and overturned, means that, in the last century, 97 per cent of UK wildflower meadows have been destroyed.

Becca's fascination with butterflies began at the age of three when her mum, Nicola, brought in a caterpillar she found on their broccoli plant. She remembers making a bed in her doll's house, watching the change from caterpillar to chrysalis, then into a small white butterfly. Finding out what to feed the small white, she provided nourishment for the adult and released the butterfly to the sky. 'It's like then and there Becca was bonded to butterflies,' her mum recounts.

Since then, Becca and her family have taken habitat restoration for these butterflies into their own hands. By introducing specific varieties, they have recorded almost a third of all species known in the UK. European peacock and small tortoiseshell caterpillars feed on the stinging nettles that the family welcome as hosts, rather than eradicate as weeds. Their adult butterflies benefit from the nectar of planted summer lilac, aptly known as the 'butterfly bush'. Becca's Butterfly Sanctuary protects eggs, caterpillars and chrysalises, alongside Becca's little sister Sarah's Butterfly Garden, which provides nectar plants for the adults. Like her sister, Sarah is equally dedicated to creating more spaces for nature and these two areas of the garden have become a true oasis of respite in a wider context of habitat loss. Such eclectic backyard spaces, blooming with flowers and shrubs of all kinds, nurtured by people like Becca and her family, are becoming new sources of thriving nature.

Yet, this is definitely not a private Garden of Eden. Becca is equally passionate about helping butterflies thrive as she is about encouraging others to do the same. She is passionate about educating and has visited her old primary school to teach about the different stages of butterfly growth and the intricacy of relationships that form between butterflies and plants. If more of us knew which plants to grow and leave in the ground, we'd be more likely to see the powdery wing of a common blue on a bird's-foot trefoil, or a brimstone hovering between the twigs of a buckthorn.

This has led to institutional change, too. Becca has led the Eco Committee at her primary school to reinvigorate its conservation area in order to make space for various species to rest, nest and reproduce. She's collaborated with regional conservation projects, sharing knowledge and passing on her homegrown food plants to create a true 'butterfly effect' of a growing world where butterflies can thrive.

Recently, a study led by the BTO found that gardens in the UK are acting as a safe haven for butterfly populations. Ignited by Becca's passion as she speaks, I wonder if more of us could provide nourishing time-outs for the painted ladies on their 9,000-mile migration from North Africa to the Arctic Circle, just by allowing more common mallow and stinging nettles to grow nearby. We don't need to wait for someone else to restore a meadow 'over there'. Small acts in small spaces can still have enormous impacts.

But, how to begin? I ask Becca. She is pensive for a moment and then tells me there are so many ways for people to start learning about and caring for wildlife. She shares one with me: everyone should go to their local nature reserve. By noticing what's around you, seeing which wings flit past you or catch your eye, 'you can go from there', research, learn and share.

Becca encourages me that 'everyone can make a difference'. Leading by example and taking care of her immediate sphere of influence, she is an example of how one person can guide others – and together re-establish this land's once thriving butterfly population.

Guardianship

PAUL POWLESLAND, RIVER RODING

Last summer, the field was a riverside meadow teeming with life. Comically tall grasses drooped with the burden of their seed heads, dusting the ground with white powder. A dizzying array of wildflowers covered a full rainbow spectrum, set among ponds of sunshine-yellow where the buttercups proliferated. A kestrel hovered overhead spying out the mice, voles and other small mammals which lived among the vegetation, unseen except for the tiny movements of the grasses signalling their presence to their hunter overhead. On sunny days I would walk barefoot, carefully picking my way through the nettles and brambles at the edge of the meadow and lie down in the sunshine, completely hidden from the world, bathed in sunlight filtered through the greenery like a stained glass window and surrounded by the heady scent of wildflowers, fresh grass and rich earth.

I was fortunate to own a tiny strip of riverbank adjacent to this meadow, which I had bought at auction from the fishing club that had managed it for fifty years. It was only a few metres across in places, sandwiched between the edge of the meadow and the adjoining River Medway. This year, I arrived at the riverbank after the spring rains with heady anticipation, ready to find out if the meadow had yet burst into life, which flowers had appeared and whether the grasses were already tall enough to hide me. Instead, I discovered the whole field had been sprayed with glyphosate. Where once there had been a verdant abundance, there was now a brittle brown expanse of nothing, giving way to a ruler-straight line of yellow where it met my land. A few weeks later I watched as the field was sliced open by the plough, and the dying remnants of meadow were sprayed with a chemical that stung my eyes and tasted of almonds. Acres of greenery, an Eden of wildflowers, the home of innumerable creatures and, above all else, life, was pulverised into a dead nothingness at the whim of an owner in search of cash crops and lucrative subsidies.

As was his right. Seeing the now bizarre contrast between his dead field and my verdant riverbank it occurred to me that it was in my power to do exactly the same. Because the name PAUL DAVID POWLESLAND was written in a government title register attached to this piece of land, it was within my power to destroy every last tree, flower, blade of grass and make all the innumerable creatures that inhabited 'my' land homeless. I could salt the earth or drench it in glyphosate to stop anything growing again, or plant invasive species like rhododendrons and cherry laurel that would escape from 'my' land to slowly destroy what was left of the dense riverside forests around me. I had the power to become a destroyer of rich, complex worlds and bring death upon its many and magnificent parts. This was a power that I knew intuitively, and felt strongly, that I should not possess.

It was perhaps fitting that the destroyed field was owned by Viscount Falmouth, who belonged to one of the oldest aristocratic families in the country. They had gained the land during the Norman Conquest: an invasion which expropriated both those living on the land and the natural world. While the subjugation of humans through the feudal system has been long abolished, the feudal subjugation of nature it ushered in largely continues, with little objection or protest.

The concept of property in the UK has been entrenched for so long as something recorded in the title register or title deed that we have forgotten that property is nothing more than a label outlining relationships. These relationships are often described as 'rights' and are both between other humans (or legal entities like companies) and with the property itself. An example of property rights between humans is the right to exclude others through the law of trespass. An example of rights in relation to the property itself is the right to use and the right to destroy, with the latter being only modestly circumscribed by environmental and planning legislation.

This idea of property as relationships becomes easier to understand when we remember that the relationship between some humans also used to be akin to one of property and ownership, and the emancipation of many peoples involved abolishing or significantly altering that relationship. We have been on a journey, lasting thousands of years, where the category of who (or what) can have legal rights has been expanded. Now, I believe, the time has come for nature's emancipation, too. The phrase 'Rights of Nature' can mean many things, from giving nature legal standing to bringing cases before the courts, to self-ownership, to specific rights enshrined in constitutions and new laws. To achieve this we need to fundamentally reimagine the way humans hold nature as property. I see two ways this reimagining might take place. The first would be to abolish the belief that we can hold nature as property in the first place, in the same way that the abolitionist movement overturned the idea that some humans could be the property of others. The second would be to retain the principle of property rights over land (and, by extension, nature) but changing the basis of that relationship into one of guardianship.

While there is an argument that some of nature should be free of any human ownership or interference, in reality most of it (especially in the UK) will have to interact with humans and cannot, by itself, speak for its own interests within a human system. This makes the first option difficult to achieve and the second more realistic. Here, one can draw an analogy with the law surrounding the protection of children.

Children were long regarded as the property of their parents or, more accurately, their father. These property rights included the right of use (as a father could demand that his children work and keep their wages) as well as a right of destruction up to a certain extent (in that a father could physically beat his children). This has now clearly changed towards a guardianship model of children, where the parent must, by law, act in the best interests of their child. There is a range of discretion given to parents to decide how they want to raise their children, but this discretion is limited, and the state can and will intervene against those parents who step outside it. Thus, a parent can decide what religion they want to raise their child in, or what hobbies they would like to support them in, but cannot severely beat them, starve them, or economically or sexually exploit them. Similarly, for landowners reimagined as guardians of nature, they could have discretion about whether to restore a piece of land as a meadow rather than a woodland, what native trees to plant or how humans can use the land in ways which are non-damaging. However, they would not be allowed to gratuitously destroy a field, or to introduce non-native trees or species, or economically exploit their land in a way that is unreasonably harmful to the natural world.

But for larger natural entities or systems (with rivers being the most obvious example) we may need guardianship bodies who can speak for its interests within our legal, economic and political systems. Although the human 'owner(s)' of the river could have a say within this body, their decision would no longer be determinative and their right to use and destroy their natural 'property' would no longer be unfettered.

Such a change in the nature of land ownership to one of guardianship may seem like a distant fantasy, but every year more and more Rights of Nature initiatives around the world are turning this fantasy into a reality. Of particular note are developments in New Zealand, where ongoing efforts to resolve the dispute between the indigenous Māori people and the British Crown have led to reimagining of the ideas of ownership of the natural world. A key issue in these disputes was the ownership of the Whanganui River. The Crown 'owned' title to the river, but the local Māori people, the Whanganui iwi, believed that the river was 'theirs', in the sense that it was a living, spiritual being to which they could trace their ancestral lineage. This dispute seemed intractable, as the Crown would not transfer ownership of the river, and the Whanganui iwi would not settle for anything less than reconnection with their ancestral river system.

The breakthrough came when it was realised that 'ownership' did not mean the same to the Whanganui iwi as it did to the Crown and to those steeped in a British legal tradition that equated ownership with dominion over nature. Instead, the Māori 'emphasise their responsibility of guardianship (kaitiakitanga) for the land to which their iwi has kinship ties. Their focus is their responsibility to care for their ancestor in order to maintain their ties to it.'[1] Both sides therefore saw a compromise which could allow both conceptions of ownership to co-exist, with the Crown retaining paper title to the river, but with an Act of Parliament[2] giving the river legal personality and a guardianship body, to consist of one representative of the Whanganui iwi and one representative of the Crown. An advisory group (known as Te Karewao) was created to provide advice and administrative support to the guardians. Of particular

importance was the creation of a new, collaborative watershed management body (known as Te Kopuka na Awa Tupua) to develop a plan to protect the health and wellbeing of the river, as well as its environmental, social and cultural interests. This body consists of different stakeholders with an interest in the river, from environmental groups, to owners, recreational users and the river itself via its guardians.

The case of the Whanganui demonstrates that it is perfectly possible for a river in an economically developed country, over which there are numerous competing rights and interests, to move from a model of ownership and dominion to one of guardianship and care. Crucially, these changes have happened in a common law legal system that is very similar to the UK. We therefore know that such changes are legally feasible and that the only obstacles to it are political.

The joy of this form of guardianship is that it goes further than merely acting as a brake on the worst excesses of the abuse of nature by those who own land. It also acts as an invitation to anyone, whether they own land or not, to step into a relationship of guardianship with the natural world. In other words, it gives everyone the opportunity to be a guardian of nature, rather than just its paper 'owners': a crucial legal step in creating a new culture of Wild Service.

Although I 'own' a piece of the River Medway, I have a deeper relationship with another river, called the Roding. This is London's third largest river, starting as a tiny trickle in a village called Molehill Green, near Stansted Airport in Essex, and ending thirty-five miles later at its confluence with the Thames in Barking. I had moved there on my boat in 2017 – becoming the first boater to live above Barking Creek – with vague ideas of mooring up and starting a community project to restore

the river. Yet over the years a slow but inexorable transformation took place. Living on and surrounded by the river, month
after month, season after season, year after year, gave rise to an
intimate knowledge of the river, its surroundings and its wildlife. This knowledge of the river, and the sheer amount of time
spent with it, produced a deep bond that over time I came to
realise was something akin to love. This love, in turn, brought
about a deep desire to protect the river from those who would
harm it and to restore it to its full beauty and magnificence.

With more connection to, and responsibility for, the river than
any of its 'owners' (or even many of those in authority tasked
with looking after it) I found myself unwittingly becoming its
guardian. All of this was without 'owning' any of the riverbed,
banks or water, or indeed with any permission from those in
authority formally tasked with looking after them. I emphasise
this in order to make it clear that anyone can choose to step into
a relationship of guardianship. The step is mental, not legal. It
can be taken without permission or a name on a title deed.

The beginning starts with connection: gaining knowledge
by spending time on or with the land or river, deepening your
relationship with it and trying to understand what it needs.
I am lucky to live on the river itself, so I not only get to see it
out of my windows, but also see many different parts of it as
I go about my life. To strengthen my knowledge further, I set
out to walk the entire river and map as many details about
it as possible. This has led to many discoveries: from the
remains of ghost rivers and culverted tributaries, to noticing
which trees thrive best in which places, to the discovery of a
colony of sand martins nesting in the river wall in the heart
of Barking. Other more depressing and mundane discoveries
include where the worst build-ups of rubbish congregate, and
where the hotspots of fly-tipping and illegal sewage spills on
the river are.

Turning this knowledge into loving and committed action is the final, crucial step. Luckily, taking it won't require much forcing, as knowing a river seems to naturally inspire a love in many people, and that love usually flows into a deep desire to protect. There are dozens of instances on the River Roding where I and other volunteers from the River Roding Trust have done exactly that. Here are just three.

One day on a volunteer rubbish-picking day at a place called the Aldersbrook (one of the Roding's tributaries), we began to smell the grim but unmistakable smell of sewage. As we looked more closely, we saw clear evidence of toilet paper lodged all along the bed of the brook. Cutting my way through brambles and nettles, I discovered a pipe was illegally discharging thousands of litres of sewage a day into the brook, as it had likely been doing for months (or perhaps longer) without anyone in authority noticing or trying to stop it. Armed with the knowledge that such illegal activity was happening, we managed to get Thames Water to monitor the adjacent sewer system for the blockages which cause the illegal discharges. We have also used the threat of legal proceedings on behalf of the river and campaigning on social media and in the press to encourage Thames Water to permanently fix the problem.

Another example concerns a landowner who dumped thousands of tonnes of building waste beside and into the River Roding in London, forming a mound of crap a kilometre long that was visible from Google Earth. Throw a tiny fraction of this amount of waste on the property of a company or government department and you would probably be arrested for criminal damage or public nuisance. Yet causing colossal damage to the natural world on your own land is almost entirely ignored by the police and the relevant authorities, even where numerous criminal offences have probably been committed. I stumbled upon the waste while walking the length of the River Roding and, trespassing onto the land to view the mound up close, I was dumbfounded by the scale and the intensity of the destruction. Although the authorities had done nothing in the six months since the waste was dumped, by photographing it and writing about it on social media I was able to gain the necessary press attention to galvanise the local authority into action. Within a couple of weeks they had issued an enforcement notice, which should hopefully see the waste removed and this stretch of the river restored to its natural state.

The last example is the most uplifting. Every year, dozens of sand martins make the perilous journey over from Sub-Saharan Africa to nest in old drainage pipes in the concrete river wall of the Roding. Seemingly oblivious to the roar of the traffic on the main road right next to them, they wheel and dive catching flies and insects over the river and adjacent Wickes Superstore without a care in the world. No one else seemed to know the martins were there; I had discovered them by chance. At first, I wasn't sure there was much I could do to help them other than cleaning their nesting holes in the winter and waiting like an anxious parent for their return from their long journey across the seas in spring. Then I found out that the owner of the adjacent land wanted to repair the river wall. They had no idea about the Barking sand martin colony and could easily have destroyed or seriously damaged its home. Taking on my role as a kind of sand martin Lorax, I spoke for them and asked for a couple of conditions: to make sure that the work was carried out outside of nesting season and that all nesting holes were replaced, with ideally a few more being added. The engineers agreed, and the sand martins continue their nesting in Barking, happily unaware that their beautifully strange and wild colony in the heart of town was ever threatened.

The right of property owners to exclude others from their land and from the natural world has robbed many of us of the

right to experience and enjoy nature. But, more importantly, it has also denied us the right to care for nature as well. I believe that humans have a deep need and longing to love and care for the natural world, and that by replacing rights of absolute ownership over nature with the idea of guardianship we can better protect it from the abusive and destructive practices that their status as mere private property often inflicts on them. In turn, we give the majority of people who do not 'own' nature the opportunity to step into a deeper and more fulfilling role as its guardian.

THE ARCHITECTURE OF BELONGING

DEN

The desire for a secret, perfect space of one's own will be familiar to most. In the childhood imagination this might be a desert island or a fairy-tale palace, but it might also be a tree house, a rock shelter, a camp or an underground hideout as cosy as the burrows of Peter Rabbit or Bilbo Baggins; as ingenious as Stig's home in the Dump; as well-provisioned as Fantastic Mr Fox's network of farm-raid tunnels. A den.

The dens built in real life might be more modest and with less risk of fatal tunnel collapse, but they are just as important. A den is a childish statement of belonging, but let's not mistake childish for trivial. Childish instincts might be the most profound we have, and denning is a deeply instinctive behaviour. A den is a place of personal safety, agency and privacy. It might also be a place of risk and self-discovery.

Den-building is an intense endeavour of vision, toil, manifestation and adaptability. The challenge is intellectual, physical, creative and often collaborative. It matters that you have to seek materials. It matters that lifting and shifting, climbing and shuttling back and forth with armfuls of branches, ferns or leaves is hard work. It matters that there is jeopardy, that the roof is only as sound as you make it. It matters that there may be splinters, scrapes or bruises. It matters that there are ethical as well as practical dimensions to resource acquisition. What components are fair game in the environment, what might be borrowed, salvaged or pilfered from other dens? In a given neighbourhood woodland there might be a steady circulation from den to den of timber poles, fragments of rope and individual logs or stumps worn smooth with age and handling.

Then, when the labour is done, there is homemaking and hospitality, and perhaps defence to consider. There might be procurement of supplies, there might even be the ultimate den-building adventure to plan ... a night sleeping out.

Den-building is a prominent part of the Forest School curriculum and is explicitly encouraged by the National Trust, which began providing dedicated areas and materials at many of their properties after listing it as one of fifty things to do before you're eleven and three-quarters. These moves highlight a rather academic recognition of denning as worthwhile, but also risk massively missing the point by turning it into a prescribed activity. A den in a place you visit on a day out is not yours. Nor is a prefab shelter packaged and sold with instructions. Because you can buy den kits now – of *course* you can – complete with badges, bunting and images of improbably clean children having fake fun, but not enough decent cordage to be useful. Nostalgia, consumerism and social anxiety combine to legitimise, sanitise, commoditise children's native wildness and curate it for learning outcomes, giftability or social media clicks.

Meanwhile, time spent in a real den is direct engagement with unvarnished mucky nature – a chance not only to observe rot and slime, beetles and worms, ants and flies, slugs and grubs, but to make a home among them. A place to brew potions and festering perfumes of foraged flowers. A place to forget when you're expected home because you are home. A den invites wonder, creativity and curiosity – at least it does if we set aside adult preoccupations for a minute or two. The best ones are hard to pass by without a peek inside and some are works of land art embellished with natural camouflage or decoration – the optics all the more magical for being ephemeral. We get lazier about denning as adults, often choosing tents, vans or bivvy bags, sometimes hanging a tarp, booking a cute Airbnb yurt, cabin or shepherd's hut instead of a self-built shelter. But crawling beneath the arch of a fallen tree, or worming into a hedge or a hawthorn thicket with a floor of beaten earth that stays perfectly dry in a rain shower engages our animal instinct in a potent way. It becomes possible to understand such spaces as sanctuaries and homes. Farmers and land managers often feel compelled to tidy these features away – to grub them out to maintain the agricultural condition of the land or reduce perceived liability. It's not a bad thing to understand what such actions, enacted on our behalf as consumers, might mean for wilder lives than ours.

Dens often get wrecked and the reasons for this vary. Some dismantlement might be carried out by rival den-builders, like birds thieving nest materials from others in a colony. Sometimes there's no real why, just the same mindless urge that makes people kick over snowmen and sandcastles. But hardest to take is the destruction by that strangest of species – the grown-up. This is intentional disenfranchisement, motivated at best by tidy-minded control-freakery or nannyish risk aversion; at worst it is outright gaslighting. 'This is not your place,' it admonishes. 'You have no rights here. We don't want it for ourselves, nor are we full of youthful angst and hormones, we just don't want you to have it.' Sometimes adults really suck.

There is something about an assertion of residency in nature that threatens establishment interests. A den is a place to experience and enact territorial instincts, and then, if we are lucky and thoughtful, to grow the hell up. Perhaps those who now disapprove of den-building never had a chance to work that stuff out when they were young, and those instincts have warped and grown into a compulsion to enclose and exclude, to other and control on a grander scale.

On the former stamping ground of the poet John Clare around the Northamptonshire village of Helpston is a stone bridge. Under one of the arches is a carving Clare made as an apprentice stonemason in 1811. In recent years this same spot also became a den-of-dens, homeliest of hovels, complete with a bed, a rack of food stores, a drawer of kitchen utensils, mantel clock and a large vase of ornamental pampas grasses. It could have been a set from Jez Butterworth's *Jerusalem*: surreal, troubling but also, to the inner child, enviable. Stumbling upon such a place invokes a strange, primal conflict – a desire to linger in what feels like homeliness and safety but also a fear of doing so, because this is a trespass more egregious than a fence climbed or a forbidden river swum. These are instincts honed by evolutionary pressures far older than humanity and certainly older than the conjuring trick of English property law. A den is a place of needful sanctuary, regardless of who owns the land on which it is built.

5

Kinship

HARRY JENKINSON, HERTFORDSHIRE

What is nature?

To some, few scenes come closer than the Yosemite Valley of California, a dramatic expanse of thick conifer forest, shielded by sheer cliffs. This National Park has come to be seen as one of the purest and most natural landscapes on earth, a 'wilderness' through and through.

But what is natural about 'wilderness' in the first place? What are the relationships hidden behind it?

In 1868, the revered great-grandfather of conservation, John Muir, set foot in the valley. This venerable sage of nature writing would go on to describe Yosemite as 'nature's landscape garden',[1] yet what was before him was thoroughly different from the tourist vista of densely packed conifers seen today. Instead, he would have seen a wide expanse of meadows, filled with groves of oak trees, animals – and *people*. For thousands of years, Yosemite had been home to indigenous peoples including the Miwuk, whose ecological practices had skilfully shaped the valley to maximise biodiversity. Through carefully burning the undergrowth, the Miwuk encouraged oaks to produce more acorns while preventing larger, devastating wildfires. Because acorns were their staple, caring for these oaks was essential. In fact, the Miwuk recognised themselves as an intrinsic part of nature as a whole. Through reciprocal relationships with the other beings of the valley, they harmonised their presence in the wider ecosystem. Non-human species were thoroughly respected – mushrooms, deer, even bears. Dances were held throughout the year to honour these great creatures as they moved through the seasons.[2] Miwuk society itself was linked to totemic systems of animals, plants and natural phenomena.[3] Overall, they maintained fundamental social connections with their fellow species through deep understandings of *kinship*.

This notion of kinship with nature is found among so many indigenous societies and sees the human situated within a wider family of beings. Anthropology teaches us that such relationality with other species is something inherently important to the human condition. It's now known that for some 95 per cent of our history, all humans were hunter-gatherers, relying directly on nature to sustain us.[4] To our ancestors, accessing nature wasn't a thing to *do*, it was permanent. You always knew you were part of nature because you relied directly on it just as children rely on their parents or other caregivers. To be human was to know kinship with the natural world.

But this relationship was almost erased, and Muir's ideas of 'wilderness' are much to blame. As colonialism forced indigenous populations off their territories, a new ideology began to dominate the land. For the colonisers, places like Yosemite were new frontiers, far from their increasingly urbanised homelands. This was another Eden where nineteenth-century white men could act out their fantasies of simultaneously showcasing and dominating nature. As historian Mark David Spence describes, 'Whenever the behavior of native people infringed on the "façade", their actions were sharply circumscribed.'[5]

For his part, Muir wrote highly racist descriptions of indigenous people in Yosemite and even described them as having 'no right place in the landscape'.[6] Rather than recognise indigenous people as the true guardians of the valley, Muir called upon the US Army to protect the area. Such dehumanising sentiments and militaristic enthusiasm helped to reinforce the horrific treatment of communities and ecologies in the colonial expansion westwards. Along with other indigenous peoples on the continent, the Miwuk were nearly wiped out through genocide, their population declining by over 96 per cent between 1770 and 1930.[7]

Yet today Yosemite has never been busier. In 2021 alone more than 3.3 million people visited the park,[8] in order to photograph the same 'empty' valley. The crowds on the viewing platforms are immense, yet every tourist cranes in to get that perfect shot of nature *without any people*. Far from preserving wildlife, the ecological health of Yosemite plummeted following the removal of indigenous people, while incidences of massive forest fires soared.[9] Today the Southern Sierra Miwuk Nation are still proudly and rightfully asserting themselves as Yosemite's guardians, but, as with other indigenous peoples, such 'fortress conservation' has left deep scars.[10] As Miwuk elder Les James stated in 2014, 'You destroyed something that we preserved for thousands of years.'[11] In a stark inversion of the truth, we have come to believe that tourists benefit wildlife but indigenous peoples do not, again internalising the lie that only the privileged can be trusted in nature. When colonisers first came to Yosemite, they shot bullets. Now they shoot photographs. But some effects are the same – the forced separation of humanity and nature, erasing people from place and kin from kin.[12]

From John Muir's idea of a peopleless landscape, conservation has unthinkingly taken up the concept of wilderness as integral to visions of ecological purity and the consequences have been devastating. In fact, the bloody history behind the picture-postcard views of Yosemite is just the tip of the iceberg when it comes to conservation's dark side. In what became known as 'The Yosemite Model',[13] the legacy of National Parks and other conservation schemes on indigenous territories has seen literally millions of people kicked off their territories. In India, the tiger-worshipping Jenu Kuruba people are being forced from their homes to make way for tiger reserves.[14] In Congo, Baka people who have spiritual relationships with their forest are being targeted by the WWF as part of a scheme for a vast 'protected area'. When they enter the forest, the Baka routinely experience arrests, acts of torture and even killings at the hands of WWF-funded rangers.[15] Colonial conservation still thrives today on severing people from their kinship with the natural world.

As Lakota chief Luther Standing Bear once stated: 'Only to the White man was nature a "wilderness".'[16]

But instead of separating indigenous peoples from nature, what if we actually listen to what they are saying? What are the lessons we can learn and apply from those who maintain the strongest ecological connections, who see our fellow species not as resources but as relations with whom we share the world?

It's important here not to homogenise or romanticise indigenous peoples. For decades, Westerners have fantasised about images of 'ecologically noble' peoples, and in doing so have homogenised millions, assuming that all indigenous peoples must wear feathers in their hair and subscribe to generic ideas of 'nature worship', without actually listening to what they were saying. Such romanticisation can go hand in hand with the pre-scription of the *right kind* of indigeneity, just as the romanticisation of nature can lead to the manipulation of a landscape to look like the *right kind* of landscape. Instead, through amplifying indigenous voices and learning from their kinship practices, we can respectfully share in a depth of ecological knowledge and reaffirm connections with our non-human kin, learning our place in nature again.

Growing up in an internationalist family, I've always been interested in societies which seemed totally different from my own.

From an early age I wanted to learn about how people lived with nature in thousands of different ways, and about their struggles to protect it. Through such interest, I have had the honour of living and working with indigenous peoples since my youth and one of the main lessons I've learned in the process is that there's nothing worse for nature than seeing human beings as separate from it. We're just as much a part of nature as the hare and the hedgehog, the otter and the owl. It's also not a superstitious belief but an evolutionary truth that your direct ancestors include other species, directly linking you back to your non-human relations. The natural world is not threatened today by who we are as a species but how our political system treats it. In Britain today, beavers are praised for their role as ecosystem engineers, creating vital biodiversity-enhancing habitats, which in turn benefit beavers. But humans are also ecosystem engineers and when we are properly connected with nature, we too know how to care for it. Around the world there are inspiring indigenous examples of such care, even in the face of the fiercest adversity.

The indigenous peoples of West Papua today are enduring a contemporary genocide under Indonesian colonial occupation, which is tearing them from their lands in the process. However, in their struggle for freedom they maintain community resilience through extraordinary connections with one another and their fellow beings. The Hubula people there have a word which encapsulates such a connection: *Etaiken*. It means heart, soul and love but translates literally as *The Seed of Singing*. Love is the source of singing and singing is an act of reciprocity deeply tied to kinship relations. To the Hubula, we are all born with a seed of singing inside us. To nurture the seeds in the soil, the Hubula sing to the nourishing plants to make them (and thereby the people) grow. This is practical. When we sing and pour out our hearts into our fellow beings, we will treat them with care. And when we do this, they will care for us.

What does such love for nature look like on a massive scale? Even the Amazon rainforest, the largest forest on earth, has been dramatically aided by human hands. The Amazon has been home to millions of indigenous people for millennia, whose ecological care has shaped the forest to an astonishing degree. The Amazon is incredibly biodiverse but it now emerges that around half of the hundreds of billions of trees there belong to just a few species and the most widespread of these are often ones cultivated and spread by indigenous communities.[17] Scientists are only beginning to realise what indigenous peoples have always known, and to understand that vast areas of the Amazon were grown by humans, in a giant reciprocal web of ecological relationships.

Today, amid a biodiversity crisis, it is no coincidence that most remaining global biodiversity is located within the territories of indigenous peoples.[18] The crises we face are also crises of disconnection, and listening to indigenous peoples leading the way towards reconnection with nature has never been more important. But interspecies relationships should not be exoticised as something only applying to peoples and lands far away. In fact, manifestations of kinship are thriving in Britain today. You just have to know where to look.

Whether it's swift box building in Lancashire, hedgehog highway projects connecting neighbours in London, or guerrilla gardening in Ceredigion, sometimes even parochial concerns seem to reveal the spontaneous human need to care for our fellow species. Even if people are not comfortable calling it kinship, you can see in certain actions the same source of grassroots care and responsibility to look after other beings. But to practise kinship, we don't need to claim indigeneity ourselves. It's not just because there have been countless migrations of people to these lands over the ages, but also because the term indigenous carries history, pain and pride behind it and should not be misused. So can we ever have a true connection to this land without being indigenous to it? Of course! Whoever you are and wherever you're from, connection is honed through relationship, not birthright; it is cultivated through non-exclusive practices of care.

We can all relearn our connections with nature. Through immersion in nature, kinship comes naturally. I'll never forget trespassing in a forest at dusk. After nervously panting up a hillside, I stopped and heard nothing but a faint drumming and, in a rush of fear and excitement, realised it was my own heartbeat. Just for a moment, it felt as though inside me was the beating heart of the forest; the animals, plants and fungi were listening and inviting me to listen back. John Berger called such moments 'forest incidents',[19] events giving us momentary timelessness amid the energy and complexity of a forest. Through such connections, we can walk alone in the woods without feeling lonely, superior or ashamed to be human but simply part of the whole.

Such 'oneness' is pragmatic. When you rely directly on nature for nourishment and shelter, you learn to protect it as a means of survival. But whether you forage your food from trees, harvest it from fields or buy it plastic-wrapped from shops, nature maintains a constant relationship with you, whether you know it or not. If we were reimmersed in nature, we would be able to see what kind of relationship this is and would work hard to heal it. But no matter how buried under centuries of feudal, capitalist and industrial disconnection from nature, we all still have seeds of singing living within us, waiting to sprout forth. We just have to listen.

In 1989, the Brazilian shaman and indigenous leader Davi Kopenawa Yanomami was invited to the UK by the campaigning organisation Survival International. The invitation was part of Davi's struggle to protect the Yanomami people from illegal gold mining on their lands. Davi's speech in the House of

Commons brought his campaign for Yanomami land rights to an international audience. Three years later, in 1992, their territory was finally demarcated, giving them much greater control over their lands.[20]

Brazilian indigenous leader Davi Kopenawa Yanomami

During his time in the English countryside, Davi mourned for our long-mistreated land, and recognised the insatiable greed which had destroyed it. He recognised it as the same force destroying his homeland, too – a force which threatened to bring a calamity the Yanomami call 'The Falling Sky'.[21]

First they started all over their own forest. Now there are few trees left on their sick land, and they can no longer drink the water of their rivers. This is why they want to do the same thing again where we live.

Davi visited the ancient stone circles of Avebury in Wiltshire. This visit, and subsequent visits to Stonehenge and other such sites in England, had a deep, enduring impact on him. Davi recognised a wisdom in the stone circles and the people who had raised them. Placing his hand on the stones, he told his British friends that while they had forgotten, their ancestors were still speaking to them and asking them to take care of the land. In his dreams, bees came to him and lamented the destruction of the forests and flowers of England. They pleaded with him to speak for them before it was too late.

> I told the white people: 'You often claim to love what you call nature. Then do not settle for making speeches, truly defend it! All its inhabitants already speak to us with the fear of disappearing. You do not see their images dance and you do not hear their songs in your dreams. Yet we shamans, we know how to listen to the bees' distress, and they are asking us to speak to you so your people will stop eating the forest.'

Will we, too, hear the bees and other beings as Davi does, as our ancestors did?

In my own village in the East of England there is a wildflower meadow near my house which has been there for perhaps over a thousand years. Not so long ago, it had been a community orchard, where villagers had planted fruit trees amid the wildflowers, nurturing themselves along with the pollinating bees – kinship in motion. Nowadays, it's fenced off and is the 'private property' of landowners who own much of the land around the village. Despite fencing off green spaces, however, they still haven't succeeded in fencing off the imaginations of wayward children. Since childhood, I've happily hopped over that fence and skipped gaily into the meadow in search of adventure. Over the years, such frolicking has transformed into guardianship. Through playing in the meadow, I came to love it and because I love it I've learned to defend it. Now as an adult, I still hop over the same fence. I wander among the cow parsley and watch the badgers, foxes and rabbits. The buzzards circle lazily while the swifts shriek with joy. Through 'trespassing' I've come to know and love these neighbours of mine for who they are. Beneath my feet, above my head and all around me, a whole ecosystem is thriving and I am part of it. These have become my kin.

In 2023, a development agency told us the game was up. The landowners, having bought the meadow several decades ago, were finally cashing in and were going to get an enormous amount for it. Huge, grotesquely expensive properties were to be built on this ancient meadow, in a village where most of my generation could never even dream of affording a house. In typical doublethink, the developer claimed that the meadow had little ecological value and that through building over it they would actually *increase* biodiversity. We have lost 97 per cent of all wildflower meadows in this country since the 1930s[22] and the pain I felt contemplating the last one in my village getting destroyed amid such blatant fallacies moved me to tears.

My village is my community and therefore also my kin. When the call to protect the meadow went up, the response was incredible. Everyone got involved with meetings and flyers and we discussed our visions for collectively looking after the meadow as a space where people and wildlife could thrive. During an onsite planning meeting, the developer stood encircled by scores of villagers from all walks of life who spoke passionately in support of the resident badgers and wildflowers. 'I hope this will make you realise what people power looks like!' said one, to a round of applause. While this is just a small parish issue, that meeting was an emotional moment. It made me realise my community extends far beyond its human inhabitants, and that when it came to it, the villagers felt the same. Nature builds bonds, not just between humans and nature but between humans and humans. Through connecting with the badgers, we connected with ourselves and reinforced a shared notion of community. Whatever happens to the meadow in the future, the impact of the experience has been profound.

The story of the meadow is not on the same scale as indigenous struggles like those in West Papua or the Amazon. But knowing my community was fighting similar battles to our forebears who resisted enclosure; knowing these systems of land grabbing were perfected in England before being exported abroad to reinforce colonial systems; knowing all that helped me to recognise a common human story. Through solidarity with one another and with the creatures of the meadow, the villagers were expressing a hidden notion which, given the chance, comes naturally to all humans – kinship.

Can we imagine a New English Countryside in which such kinship is applied on the grand scale? The Potawatomi botanist Robin Wall Kimmerer envisages a 'democracy of species', whereby 'We recognize the beingness of each other, the personhood of each other, and that we all have a right and a responsibility and a gift to bring to the whole.'[23] Only through imagining such alternatives can we begin to create the space for them to happen, and to reweave ourselves and our kin back into the same tapestry of a thriving community. And this needs to be extended globally, not through coloniality but through solidarity; respecting the rights of every community and valuing their care over every green space. When we view ourselves as part of a living web of beings rather than outside of it or on top of it, our relationship with one another changes from one of exploitation to one of reciprocity. To truly care about the natural world, we have to feel the living, breathing connections of life and recognise the inherent value and meaning in all beings, human and non-human.

With kinship, we nurture the cultures of care in all of us. We grow seeds both outside us and within us and, when we do, we let our hearts sing.

WILD SERVICE IN ACTION

HEIDI AND THE PEOPLE POPULATING POPLARS

If trees were creatures, black poplars would be pandas. Endangered, charismatic and bad at getting laid, the British variant of the black poplar now mostly requires human intervention in order to survive. Once a staple of our landscape, their numbers have diminished to the point of rarity, as the winter-flooded meadows and riparian plains they love have been drained, and their strong, hardy wood has seen them hacked down for timber. Worse, those that are left have ceased to sexually regenerate. And nobody is quite sure why.

'Nobody has come up with an answer yet but we have a number of hypotheses,' says Dr Heidi Hauffe, a conservation geneticist based in San Michele all'Adige, Italy, whose new project hopes to map the British poplar population's genotype in more detail than ever before. Out-of-sync flowering times, fertility loss through hybridisation, simple age, or the distance between differently gendered trees, are all possible explanations. For the latter, a certain British priggishness may be to blame: the females of the species are prone to producing vast quantities of unseemly white fluff, which may have encouraged their felling by scandalised landowners. The result is that in most of Britain there now aren't enough trees of both sexes in the right places to sexually reproduce, making them reliant on vegetative spread (reproduction from offshoots) to propagate instead.

Black poplars are beautiful. Tall and expansive, with fissured trunks pockmarked by burrs and bosses, you can pick them out on the horizon thanks to their melancholy lean and the way their bark glows orange in a low spring sun. Once, the trees were our land markers, distinguishing the boundaries between parish and county. They lived alongside us for generations, drawn especially to soggy commons, ponds and village greens. Look closely and you'll even spot them in the background of Constable paintings. Now, across Britain there are only around 7,000 left, making them our rarest native hardwood.

'They have amazing characters,' says Heidi when I ask what draws her to the tree. 'They have so many different shapes and big lenticels ... the more you look at them the more you realise they're so characteristic of the landscape and an important part of the community of the forest.' Their niche-forming bark also makes them especially good habitats for species like owls and bats.

Yet, somehow, the black poplar's fate has been ignored. As Richard Mabey notes in *Flora Britannica*, 'It is astonishing that such a conspicuous species should have passed so thoroughly out of common knowledge.' Its fortunes have been kept alive through the perseverance of two generations of professional botanists and the enthusiasm of a small pool of amateurs who, recognising the tree's value, propagate it wherever they can find pockets of habitat left.

That's essential. Because what remain of the species in Britain are, for the most part, living a spectral present: relics of a 'wilder and wetter landscape' which are now only capable of regenerating through human intervention, achieved by the removal of small branches from extant trees to be planted around the country.

Easily done, you might think. But it ain't so simple. Crucial to the tree's prospects is the maintenance of its genetic diversity. That's essential for its long-term resilience, especially as climate change makes conditions ever more uncertain, and pathogens akin to those which have afflicted the elm and ash proliferate in other species. Genetic diversity ensures there's enough range within the species to future-proof against such risks, and ensures too that genotypes adapted to different climatic and environmental conditions (known as 'ecotypes') survive.

Initial sampling of the British black poplar has identified as many as eighty-seven variants. Yet the distribution of the variants ... varies. The top five most frequent genotypes account for over 66 per cent of all the trees in a given sample, with the other eighty-two genotypes distributed within the remaining 33 per cent. Likewise, their spread is geographically limited, with twenty-two of the counties included in the sample only containing a single sex of tree. The consequence is that large parts of the tree's gene pool are at risk of dying out.

In steps Heidi, who hopes to deepen our understanding of the poplar's gene pool in order to work out which clones have the greatest genetic diversity. These can then be used to stock clone banks for use around the country. Her work builds on that of the British botanists Ken Adams and Edgar Milne-Redhead, who over successive generations surveyed the black poplar and began the genetic mapping process. Their research, combined with this new, fine-tuned genetic analysis, creates the necessary scholarly foundation for a mass rollout of black poplar recovery.

But to succeed, it cannot happen in isolation. A growing network of amateurs have begun taking up the tree's cause, drawing on the guidance of the professionals to source genetic rarities and distribute them where they ought to belong, such as along the River Roding in East London, where Paul Powlesland acts as guardian. He believes:

> I really see this as open to anyone ... I don't think it needs a professional nursery approach. In one day you could create ten new versions of the rarest kind of trees in the UK, with very little training required. It seems like the perfect example of grassroots action for nature.

Heidi shares his optimism.

> There's no doubt there is a great culture of trying to preserve nature as a volunteer in the UK. Being out in nature. Saving nature. Volunteering many many hours for it, even until a late age ... it's hugely energising, because the passion that comes out and the willingness to learn and exchange information, the openness to collaborate – that's very UK!

With a little coordination, a network of such amateurs could begin working from the centralised register that the work of scholars like Ken Adams and Heidi has helped create, documenting when cuttings have been taken and where they've now gone; steadily building rare iterations of the tree to a healthy threshold of recovery. In so doing, they will bridge a gap that nature can no longer bridge itself; a collective healing which sutures past disregard in the hope of a new, more abundant future.

6

Reciprocity

AMY-JANE BEER, DERWENT VALLEY

'That which is given in submission becomes a
medium of defiance'
— Sumerian proverb, c.1900 BCE

There's an apple tree outside our house. We planted it four-teen years ago and now it produces rosy fruit in such bough-bending abundance that short of hauling the lot off to a juicing service we can't use them all ourselves. And so, when they are ready each September, we put up a sign inviting passers-by to share. Windfalls are left for the birds, rabbits, squirrels and voles; bruised fruits serve as insect pubs where beetles, butter-flies, wasps and flies booze and snooze.

Over Yule we decorate the branches with ribbons, bells and baubles — nothing remotely coordinated or tasteful — then dowse them with mulled cider and song, willing the tree to life and fur-ther productivity. Last year a meteor shower added celestial bling to the occasion, to squeals of delight from adults and children alike.

A few weeks later I was bringing the decorations down when a couple stopped to ask if I was 'the lady who gives us apples'. I said I was, they thanked me and went on their way. I continued unhooking the baubles, untying the ribbons, then came to an uneasy stop. Something was wrong.

Most of us know that awkward feeling when somebody has given too generously, or when we have not reciprocated adequately. A gift is something offered freely with no explicit expectation of return, but however generously meant it also comes with something else: a soft power that settles on the recipient. A gift unreciprocated is a loose end; an imbalance; a dishonour – a literal embarrassment of riches. It's so uncomfortable that an entire pointless gift industry exists to exploit our anxiety, helping us give cheaply and conveniently, while completely missing the point.

The disarming power of a gift was explored at length by Marcel Mauss almost a century ago, in what was to become a seminal anthropological text. In *The Gift*, he invoked a Māori term, *hau*, for the spirit or force inherent in a thing given. Explicit in Māori wisdom is an understanding that this force also exists when the giver is not human, and thus binds people in obligation to non-human nature as well as to each other. *Hau* exists in order to prevent us cheating the system on which we depend by taking more of nature's abundance than we need, or by failing to reciprocate. *Hau* places a moral and social obligation on the recipient to return excess, actually or symbolically, for example by releasing a proportion of trapped birds, by scattering woodchips from harvested timber back into the forest, or by putting some of the garnered abundance beyond human use through ritual destruction, deposition or regifting to the non-human realm.

As a student of biology in the early 1990s, I first encountered reciprocity in the context of animal behaviour, where it was invoked cautiously to explain why animals might help each other. Altruism, defined as behaviour that incurs a cost to the donor while benefiting the recipient, presented a particular challenge to the development of Darwin's theory of evolution by natural selection because any characteristic that reduces individual fitness (measured purely in terms of gene flow into future generations) is likely to dwindle in a population over time. And yet clearly such behaviours happen – organisms often invest time, energy or resource in others, for example by grooming each other, by sharing food or engaging in protective behaviour. Darwinism required that the costs of such giving were balanced or exceeded by benefits that increase reproductive success.

The considered view of behaviourists and evolutionary biologists was that altruism could only happen if the donor and recipient were related (so-called kin selection) or if the donor was reliably repaid (reciprocal altruism), reducing the effective cost to zero over time. In both cases the investment would pay off in terms of increased flow of genes (from the donor individual or from close relatives with highly similar genotypes) to the next generation: in other words, the generosity meant more babies.

Social reciprocity might be direct (help one who has helped you), indirect (help one who helps others) or generalised (help anyone if you are helped, regardless of who you were helped by). Both direct and indirect reciprocity were thought to require too much social cohesion and cognitive processing power (recognising other individuals and keeping account of who owes what) to occur in anything other than 'high functioning' social species such as primates. Generalised reciprocal altruism was considered 'easier' in terms of processing and was used to explain the behaviour of vampire bats, which appear to willingly share food with hungry but unrelated members of a colony.

What about reciprocity across species boundaries? The definition of a species is a genetically isolated group, so why help a competitor from an entirely different gene pool? Why, for example, would a humpback whale or dolphin rescue another species from orca attack? Rigid Darwinism could only interpret such selfless interventions as inadvertent altruism by animals that just can't help themselves from helping. As long as an ability to empathise is sufficiently beneficial in terms of kin selection or reciprocal altruism, it could be allowed the odd misfire. Humans, with our prodigious capacity for empathy, had to be regarded as a special case.

Then we discovered the Wood Wide Web: the fungal network through which plants, organisms with no nervous system, let alone brain, share resources with others *of the same and different species* via networks of mycorrhizal fungi, donating in some seasons, drawing down at others. A healthy plant in a sunny spot, well supplied with water and micronutrients, might easily find itself with way more carbohydrate by photosynthesis than it can use or store. To such an individual, the giving isn't really a cost, but a sharing of this abundance.

Ah. This sounds familiar. It sounds a lot like *hau*.

I realise that *hau* is what I'm feeling now, standing by the apple tree on a January morning, clutching a handful of damp ribbons and bells, and grasping, not for the first time, but perhaps in a new way, that the abundance of nature is a gift. I want to run up the lane to find the couple who'd thanked me and explain, breathlessly, that I misspoke. That I don't own this living, giving being. That we just brought it here to live by us. But then I think I'd also have to explain that the tree is in a similar relationship with the fungi tending its roots and another with the pollinators that visit its flowers, and which, many years ago, serviced the blossom of its parents. It is indebted to all the lives that accumulated organic matter, then regifted it to create the unique physicochemical matrix of soil in this one spot. It owes the rain and the sun. I'd need to explain that some of those debts were settled in pollen and sugary nectar and fruit, some paid forward to us. That it is all part of an overall balance sheet that makes the global financial system look primitive and clunky.

I'd have to say that we can't step out of the deal because our biologically defining characteristic as human animals is that we are consumers, but that we're really just borrowing it. Every atom of matter, every joule of energy. We are compost in waiting.

Our desire to reciprocate can make us vulnerable to exploitation – not so much in natural selection any more, but in its economic analogue. It's no surprise that capitalism has found a way to make giving back a business – trading in debts to nature through offsetting schemes, carbon credits and 'micro consumerist bollocks', as George Monbiot calls it. The economist Ernst Friedrich Schumacher wrote that 'Any intelligent fool can make things bigger, more complex, and more violent. It takes a touch of genius and a lot of courage to move in the opposite direction.' Can we do that? Can we simplify our urge to reciprocate?

If we accept that nature's account book can stretch to encompass all life as kin, things do start to seem more simple. This view of kinship is much less granular and quantitative than that of rigid Darwinism and sees reciprocity not so much as a transaction but part of an all-embracing cycle.

Many societies specify startlingly convergent codes of reciprocity, with basic requirements to *introduce yourself*; to *ask*; and to *show gratitude* for what we consume. It is for good reason that *hello*, *please* and *thank you* are usually the first words we learn in a new language.

In *Braiding Sweetgrass*, the botanist and indigenous wisdom keeper Robin Wall Kimmerer uses the example of foraging wild leeks, a seasonal spring delicacy and cousin of our ramsons or wild garlic, to describe how the code works in the context of foraging.

Introducing yourself, Kimmerer explains, brings accountability. It calls us to accept personal responsibility for our actions, to not waste what we have taken, to give in return. Asking requires a clear understanding of what will be taken and the

effects on species, communities or systems we are taking from. This understanding demands that we take only what we need, that we leave more than we take and that we minimise harm: for example, never taking the first or the last of anything, avoiding impacting systems under particular stress. Asking also requires us to accept when nature's answer is no. In Kimmerer's example the first leeks she digs up are withered where the fat bulbs should be, which she takes as a clear signal to wait as long as it takes for abundance to be restored. Showing gratitude means giving in return, sharing, sustaining the ones that sustain us, and stepping up to celebrate, educate and advocate.

Gratitude may feel like the very least form of reciprocity. But, like giving, it holds a hidden power. It reminds us of our dependency but can also feel like a second gift. The word is thought to have its etymological root in a 5,500-year-old proto-Indo-European verb *gwerə* – meaning 'to favour' or 'to praise', which also flows into *agree*, *grace* and, intriguingly if less obviously, into *bard* – a reminder that gratitude is celebratory. It is not the same as payment or penance.

Receiving should be restorative, and when we are restored we can give in any number of ways. In the modern context those ways might be collecting litter, recording wildlife, teaching, campaigning, writing letters, planting and tending trees or wildflowers, creating habitat, but they might also include offerings of song, story, art, prayer or deep attention.

I give my attention to the apple tree. A familiar muse, not least for its multifaceted, complex and deliciously contradictory symbolism. The fruits are seen as wholesome (the health-giving apple a day to keep the doctor away), common and affordable, if not free. But then there are concocted ideas of temptation and forbidden fruit, exoticising and prejudicing an otherwise perfect example of cross-species reciprocity. When we eat an apple, then lob the core, or spit or shit the seeds into a thicket or a woodland clearing, we're doing what the tree wants. Given a choice it would favour the latter, as partial digestion aids germination and manure is a parting gift of nutriment. This relationship is why fruits like apples exist. Why they ripen to colours that draw our eye. Why the tree invests in sugars it will not consume itself – to sweeten deals with pollinators and seed dispersers. The serpent showed Eve what the garden needed from her. The forbidden fruit was freighted with power, but the power wasn't original sin. It was original magic. Old Wow. Old *hau*.

I love the ferality of apple trees. They have been select-ively propagated for centuries, but never wholly domesticated. We've selected for sweetness, crunchiness, colour, storability, texture when raw or cooked, but if an apple seed germinates and the seedling grows to maturity, its fruit may bear no resem-blance to that which the seed came from. Like us they exhibit what geneticists call 'extreme heterozygosity', which is to say they are wildly individualistic.

To get the fruit we want we must pay it forward, grafting twice over: first the horticultural graft, welding cutting to root-stock; second the graft of labour to plant, water and care for the tree and its setting – bare or broken ground is needed to limit competition. In the wild this groundbreaking service might be provided by hogs or badgers, but orchard trees are usually started off in a nursery before being transplanted.

Traditionally managed, organic orchards are astonishingly biodiverse. Alongside hedgerows and wood pasture, with which they often intermingle, they are perhaps the closest thing to the wild wood of post-glacial, pre-agricultural Britain. This was not a land of closed canopy forest, but a mosaic of woodland, scrub and glade disturbed and disrupted by large herbivores: short-tusked elephants and beavers, aurochsen and deer. Their crashing and smashing, felling and clipping constantly rebooted the processes that bring ecological rejuvenation and diversity.

Traditional management such as coppicing and hedge-laying replicates these interventions, less chaotically than nature would, but resulting in a similar mix of wildwood elements.

Trees growing in a relatively open habitat, be it an orchard or a wildwood mosaic, tend to develop more stable, spreading forms than they would in closed canopy forest, because they don't face such an urgent race for the light in their early years. They therefore live longer and develop more old-age features such as rot holes, hollow trunks and standing dead wood, which add greatly to their biodiversity value. Decaying wood supports fungi and the larval stages of myriad invertebrates, which in turn attract species that feed on them. Rot holes and crevices provide secure nesting, roosting and caching sites for birds, bats and other small mammals, and even toads climb into tree holes and hollows, where food in the form of slugs and grubs comes to them. Orchard species such as apples, pears and plums have a tendency to develop veteran features early, at around fifty years old. Thus even a new orchard, managed appropriately, can become an exceptionally rich habitat within just a couple of human generations, as long as the humans are there to help.

The biodiversity of traditional orchards includes specialist species like the noble chafer beetle, a large metallic-green insect whose larvae spend three years developing in the dead heart-wood of fruit trees, but which as adults need sunlit edges and open spaces where hogweed, meadowsweet and elder grow. The large, pale, umbelliferous flowering heads of such species provide nectar, pollen and conspicuous platforms on which to court and mate. For these jewel-like creatures, closed canopy forest won't do, and the remaining population in England and Wales is associated principally with traditional orchards.

We have lost 90 per cent of these habitats in England since the 1950s. Only a tenth of those remaining are fit to provide a long-term habitat and almost half are in declining condition – principally because new trees are not being planted as old ones die. Replacement is vital in maintaining age structure so that the full range of microhabitats is maintained. It's not only biodiversity we're losing. There are more than 2,500 varieties of apple recognised in England. Each has a heritage value of its own, but only a handful are widely known or consumed. Until recently the folk culture of orchards was dwindling, too, including the tradition of wassailing – a rambunctious invocation of life in the darkest part of year, with midwinter carolling, carousing, feasting and drinking, fire-making and offerings of toast and cider to the trees. Fortunately, the tide is turning. A concerted national effort to map and survey traditional orchards and network community projects has struck a chord. Old orchards are being restored, new ones planted and many are managed for wildlife, or as gathering places, with pizza ovens and picnic tables, serving a function somewhere between playground and pub, and wassailing is back. It turns out orchards are about so much more than apples.

I think of the noise and revelry of the wassail, a festival of reciprocity as potent as any we might look to indigenous cultures elsewhere to provide. Perhaps we do still know how to do this. I think of the sweets, flowers, fruits and grains presented at the festivals and shrines of almost all religions; of the many rituals of symbolic sacrifice and votive offering: carved antler points and exquisite stone axe heads in wetlands; bronze weapons in rivers; coins in fountains and wishing trees. Gifts, given back.

Were they intended for gods or for nature herself? What if they are the same thing?

They are, whispers the apple tree. *We are. We are the same thing.*

Reciprocity can be the work of a moment or a life, but attention to the former tends to become the latter and really there's not so much difference between the two. Time is big. I get a sense of bio-vertigo and self-dissolution when trying to feel my place in the interconnected mesh of life, the vastness of space or the enormity of geological time. As Robert Macfarlane wrote, 'you learn yourself to be a blip in the larger projects of the universe. But you are also rewarded with the realisation that you do exist – as unlikely as it may seem, you do exist.' And for that, I am simply grateful. For that, I will be happy to spend my days relearning those gestures of reciprocity; and for that I will be glad one day, to give it all back.

I don't run up the lane. I do a little dance in the weak sunshine with the ribbons and bells, as I like to think Darwin himself might if he were alive, because I can't imagine he'd mind that those advancing his own revelatory thinking sometimes trip up over other equally beautiful ideas. Then I bring the decorations indoors, dry them on the boiler and put them away for another year.

Reading

Kimmerer, Robin Wall, *Braiding Sweetgrass: Indigenous Wisdom, Scientific Knowledge and the Teachings of Plants*, Milkweed Editions, Minneapolis, 2013

Mauss, Marcel, *The Gift: Forms and Functions of Exchange in Archaic Societies*, 1925, most recent translation Jane I. Guyer, Hau Books, Chicago, 2016

Schumacher, Ernst Friedrich, *Small Is Beautiful: A Study of Economics as if People Mattered*, Blond & Briggs, London, 1973

Monbiot, George, 'Capitalism is killing the planet, it's time to stop buying into our own destruction', *Guardian*, 30 October 2021

Hamilton, William Donald, 'The genetical evolution of social behaviour', *Journal of Theoretical Biology* 7 (1) 1964, 1–16

Maynard Smith, John, 'Group Selection and Kin Selection', *Nature* 201 (4924), 1964, 1145–7

https://ptes.org/campaigns/traditional-orchard-project/

WILD SERVICE IN ACTION

MARGARET AND MAY MOSS BOG

It's mid-spring in the North York Moors National Park and the ground is sodden underfoot. In the distance, tiny lanterns of powder-pink flowers dangle at the tip of a small oval-leafed stem. The silence invites curlews to nuzzle into this year's nests, some returning to their spots from last year, other pairs finding new places to roost. The deep, moist scent of the earth rises up through the wings of an emperor moth as it flutters over a slithering adder, coiling along with its tongue out, seeking a mate. May Moss is the largest single area of blanket bog on the North York Moors. 'It's fed by rainwater only,' Margaret

Atherdon tells me. She and her colleagues have been studying these soaked peaks for the last forty years, monitoring the vegetation and rainfall fluctuations. This unique water flow, along with the historic inaccessibility of the site — devoid of grazing cattle and restricted to researchers and soldiers — makes May Moss an incomparable place to study climate change.

Globally, natural peatlands cover 3 per cent of the earth, but hold nearly 30 per cent of all soil carbon, more than double that of all forests. Their absorptive ability means they hold water up in the highlands, reducing flood risks for nearby settlements. Not only that, but they support a huge variety of life: wading birds like dunlins come to breed and threatened birds of prey, like hen harriers, fly less than five metres above the ground to hunt in the soggy shrubs.

So, why has access here been so peculiar? May Moss sits next to Fylingdales Airspace, a bizarrely shaped obelisk at the top of the hillside. Previously a nuclear missile detection centre, the base now monitors changes in space junk. Margaret says that access 'wasn't easy during the late 1960s'. She had been collecting cores of the deep-earth at various sites in the area and analysing the ancient pollen granules for her PhD in vegetation history at Durham University. Public hysteria about nuclear and radioactive cows had led all farmers to remove their animals in the early 1960s, leaving an expanse of silent and scattered peat bog around the base.

On one such pollen collection day, as she walked back through the dense sphagnum moss (*Sphagnum spp.* — a genus of plant able to hold twenty times its weight in water), Margaret's eye glanced across at a flush of pale pink amidst the brown vegetation. Dick Bell, Head Warden of the North York Moors at the time, had asked Margaret to look out for one particular species, called bog rosemary. There had been old records of growth in the area, but no one had seen any for years. She drew out the rolled leaves and blushing flowers in detail, learning what to look for before scouring the area. Eventually, she and a colleague found what they had hoped for: a spread of bog rosemary growing, appropriately, in the middle of the bog. But that was not the only discovery. As they continued to explore, her colleague Dunstan Adams from the Yorkshire Wildlife Trust yelled, 'Great Scot!' His gaze was fixed on the palm-shaped, light green leaf of a cloudberry – one of Britain's rarest plants. It led to the first wave of protection for May Moss and a section of the bog was officially designated an SSSI.

The ecological diversity in peatlands is huge, with some wetland habitats showcasing '118 plants and 214 species of invertebrates, birds and mammals within 1km',[2] according to the International Peatland Society. Dense wetlands like May Moss are found mainly at higher altitudes and other places with low temperatures and lots of rain. Peatland soils build up over many years as deoxygenated decomposition of plant matter builds up year after year, generating around one metre of peat every 1,000 years. However, despite peatland cover spanning approximately 12 per cent of the UK, peatlands are in shocking condition. Only 20 per cent of these remain in a healthy condition, the remainder suffering mismanagement in the form of overgrazing, agriculture and timber plantations that require drainage, atmospheric pollution and copious amounts of burning, construction and extraction of peat for horticulture.

Margaret's botanical attention to detail and the skills that led to the protection of May Moss had developed through exposure to different plant environments. Her passion for peatlands felt infectious and made me want to understand the wealth of relationships within these soggy realms. 'People are important,' she tells me. They can monitor and notice changes which can influence policy and provide more protection for nature. Margaret reminds me of the 2010 review 'Making space for nature', which emphasised the need for 'bigger, better and more joined up wildlife sites'. Such early and regular interaction with nature is essential to develop the interest, skills and breadth of knowledge which can produce a new generation of Margarets across England.

That's why she doesn't believe ecology should be restricted to the ivory tower. She runs PLACE (People, Landscape And Cultural Environment) of Yorkshire, a re-engagement project which provides short courses and field trips to facilitate reconnection to nature for everyday people. The ability to recognise differences between the living things around us is a skill innate to us all; it just takes someone to ignite the spark. Once we choose to hone in our focus, our eyes will naturally sharpen to new patterns in the undergrowth. With just a snippet of attention, an intricate tree of life starts to unfold in front of us. These observational skills, long lost but easily returned, need nurturing if we want to restore these globally extracted habitats.

In positive news, the past few decades have seen attitudes towards nature conservation evolve, especially towards peatlands. Along with individuals like Brian Walker, the ecologist for the Forestry Commission who led the way towards the felling of timber plantations, people like Margaret have been advocating for restoration for the wildlife on this bog with a multitude of approaches over the years. She remembers going along with someone from Natural England to block up the drains herself, stuffing bits of peat in the holes that were dug previously to dry out the peatland. Today, two formerly separate peat basins have reconnected over the interfluvial ridge and merged into a 370-acre blanket bog.

So, May Moss continues to expand. It is home to an increasing bounty of flora and fauna: meadow pipits and cross-leaved heather often call this land home. Common snipe roam freely over the ridge and emerald damselflies dart across the shrubs. And it's not just the life in the uplands that's recovering. In the valley below, the plugging of peatland pipes means more water is held up high and the flood risks in towns, like nearby Pickering, have decreased substantially − from 25 to 4 per cent in any given year. Responsible care and understanding of our broader biome means peatlands like these can be restored successfully to create flourishing, sphagnum-filled, waterlogged wetlands and natural flood defences.

Margaret is a clear example of how individual our relationships with different landscapes need to be. By giving attention to the world, we notice its intricacies and how each unique habitat contributes to the wider biome. May Moss is a triumph for wildlife, near and far, showing the importance of widespread restoration of peatlands. The more we can distribute the skills of care and attention through projects like PLACE, the more likely it is we will one day see many more of these highland sponges restored, coated in sporadic flushes of pink haze.

7

Community

NICOLA CHESTER, WEST BERKSHIRE

Community is one of the most powerful ideas (or instincts) we have ever had as a species. The thought that the common *place*, and the things we have in common, can bind us all together — as something that entwines, supports, connects and brings along with it (like wild clematis or honeysuckle through a hedge) is extraordinarily common in itself. It is a concept full of hope and possibility in these times of multi-crises.

At its root, the Latin *communitatem* stands for fellowship and a union of common ownership, where to 'own' is to take initiative and responsibility. It embraces relations, feelings and actions based on friendly engagement, inclusion, courtesy and respect. The old English *gemænscipe* (something in social possession, common interest or enjoyment) has a similarity to the word yeomanship, itself descended from the word *geaman*, a villager or commoner who cultivates the land: a humble, faithful, useful servant. By the sixteenth century, community was a 'commonty' of land held by its people, in service – and from there we might gather the threads of intention that a community is as much a faithful service to the land and its wild inhabitants as its people.

But too often, when we talk about community we exclude the wild element: we forget the plants, the insects, the butterflies, spiders and birds, the soil bacteria. We even talk about communities of plants and animals, and don't include ourselves, even though we share, one way or another, the same habitat. This communal habitat may be one of myth, story or association; it may be food, farming and foraging, sanctuary or freedom. But it is nothing without the land.

Where I live, the downland, heathy commons, arable fields and sheep walks of north Wessex, might seem like relatively remote, unpeopled countryside, but they are full of the stories of human engagement (as any locality will be) with the land. The seed-drilled, corduroy-combed fields, the silky, moving pelt of flowing crops – all beneath a raining sky of larks – are lines drawn and redrawn over the body of the land, over and again, following the same curves families and whole villages would have known. It is the same for urban parks and commons. And all this is space shared by our wild neighbours. The brown hare resting in those soft, working, corduroy folds; the peregrine that marks the woodcock migrating over the city at night, uplit by the streetlamps we walk under. Neighbours. Of all kinds.

There is memory of community in the land, right up to this moment. It may be the shared effects of weather or climate change; it may be the memory of tillage, walks to school or all the things that happen communally on playing fields, 'recs' and village greens. It could even be the shared effects of pollution, or the surnames on the war memorial, the legacy of something once inflicted whose memory lingers on. There are myriad and diverse threads between us, from acts of love to the air we breathe, the bacteria in the dust beneath our feet, the symbiotic filters between us. We are all made of stardust and the rain from summer lightning or last year's snow. Our cells come and go quicker than morning dew, or the leaves on the trees. We are more weather pattern and environment than we are 'just' a human body. Every leaf, feather, glittering beetle wing case, line on the palm of a hand – this planet, this life, is a miracle of community. It's the key to everything, and, particularly now, to all our joined up, interconnected futures.

Too often we don't see it this way. We've been putting a distance between ourselves and nature for a long and deeply damaging time. Most of us don't know what farming goes on in the neighbouring fields, or can make the connection (if there even is one) with the food we buy. We accuse farmers of wholesale wildlife destruction, without putting ourselves or the communal notion of 'policy' in the picture. We fence ourselves off and allow others to fence us out, like docile, compliant livestock. Our understanding and engagement is pushed to the edges, as well as our access, as if we cannot be trusted, or be responsible – and that is how a community gets broken. We need to widen the brief of that *communitatem*; that yeomanship.

Over and through that same downland landscape of my home, rich with peopled stories, the wild clematis and its many names – old man's beard, traveller's joy, tuzzy-muzzy, skipping ropes or bedwine (as it's known locally) – twines and tangles through everything: the boundaries, scrub, former commons and hedgerows, wandering along lost and existing byways, with a certain ghostliness and alchemy of its own. It has become something of a motif and waymarker for me and, of course, has a community of its own. The almond-scented flowers that attract bees, hoverflies and moths, the twisted vines you can swing from, and the tiny, moth-antennae plumes of the 'achenes' of seeds (miniature purls of ostrich feathers!) appear betwixt and between, rambling unruly for long stretches, seeding itself, appearing and disappearing mysteriously with the weather and the light. It partners with other members of its wayfaring, track-marking community: guelder rose and elder, whitebeam and crab apple, spindle, honeysuckle and the wayfaring tree itself. Yet another name, 'woodbine' lends itself to one of the oldest (and cheapest) brands of cigarettes. Favoured by the working classes, the name is a reference to the rural habit of smoking sections of the twisted vine itself. The plant in winter suggests smoke – and a back and forth of language between us.

I am haunted a little by those voices of the rural past. But I am haunted more by the catastrophic losses of farmland birds and wildlife – I see them sometimes like a vivid, cinematic overlay on the blank page of an empty sky – and I am haunted by the loss of knowledge, too; of inequality of access to nature, of shifting baseline syndrome, nature deficit disorder, and the nature disconnection which is at the heart of the biggest crisis we've ever faced as a species and the disastrous decisions we continue to make.

Sometimes, in this rural working community, those voices are loud and living echoes of a world not quite lost – for good and bad. I am a keen listener to the ghosts of an old order of things, but it is crucial to be en garde against rose-tinted nostalgia and tradition that can be coercive or exclusive, unwilling to embrace, perceive or listen to anyone else's views. Rural communities were often poor and isolated and their attitude to nature not much different from ours now. But there was a bounty that is going, gone now. When we weren't looking, that sense of separation cost us our relationship with nature in many ways, taking a toll on us physically, mentally and societally. The countryside is emptying of workers on the land, and it is emptying of wildlife, too. Only a very few people are engaged in either, and it seems communication and community exist in vacuums between them.

The emptying countryside has far more to offer than land to invest in, second homes (empty for half the year), old cottages to extend, do up and Airbnb, and the rural dream of estate agent windows. Yet in so many areas it is in danger of becoming a ghetto of wealth and privilege where residents bemoan the lack of facilities or 'trades' to employ, because they've priced them out: schools, shops, pubs and clubs close, because there's no one to work in or use them. Plumbers and decorators, farriers and carers, paramedics, teaching assistants, gardeners and cleaners come in from outside, to service the houses they grew up in. And what of the Scout leaders, babysitters, pantomime and choir leaders, village market and fête organisers, school governors, storytellers, beekeepers and artists? Evict or drive out rural tenants, diversity and community players to your own detriment. But celebratory events and gatherings prove a strong but gentle resistance to the steady dismantling of communities through ownership and wealth that does not consider a place's people, history, change for good, or its particular, unique magic.

Fêtes and community halls become a renewed focus for a kind of social barn-raising, where funds are raised, raising the roof in social gatherings, over and over, for different community needs: lockdown laptops for children without tech to access pandemic home schooling, barn dances to support Ukrainian refugees, a children's play area or a new pavilion. The partying, dancing and ceilidhing still happens with gusto, as do merry moonlit walks back through fields and woods afterwards, along ancient shortcuts and desire lines back to homesteads.

Facebook and WhatsApp groups become new sources for mutual aid and knowledge-sharing from enquiries to where the tea urn went, to offers of help when someone has a new baby, or questions over what the crop is growing in the field behind the village hall, who has heard the cuckoo first, or through those things that test people 'in common' to pull together: Covid, water shortages and power outages, road closures or snow, or the felling of a much-loved copse. These are things that Flora Thompson would recognise, in her semi-autobiographical trilogy of post-enclosure, working-class memoirs, *Lark Rise to Candleford*.

There is delight and celebration in these fêtes and 'junketings', but to stay alive and relevant, they must invite and embrace

change, too. We need urgent social change for the times ahead, of the times here now, and we can do it by extending and rewriting our community narrative and accountability.

It has to include nature from all quarters. And nature *can* bring us together from often deeply entrenched positions on what nature is to us and who it 'belongs' to. By enclosing and excluding others, we cut ourselves off. Rural work is increasingly lonely work, and with the pubs and 'chatter alleys' of the farmworkers' cottages gone, negative rumination is often rife – when we could be outward looking, inviting others to understand, celebrate work and share knowledge. We've more in common than we know, including the ability to learn from each other.

Some of the community-spirited ghosts I tune into are two queer women, Marguerite de Beaumont and her partner Doris Mason, and their friend, Julia White, who farmed here in the forties and fifties. They made progress and embraced change, advancing their farms from horse to tractor and coping with a diminishing workforce, but brought the community with them; they challenged the status quo, sought input from those that worked for them, listened and improved things, referring all the time to their community. They involved them (not just when needed at harvest) but in Scout and Guide groups, the Women's Institute, church and school, the ubiquitous fêtes and celebrations – and, crucially, in the stories they told and recorded, too, in notes that remain, diaries published, and in memories still held by the village referencing the past, with an eye firmly on the future.

Sharing the stories of a place through time (the personal and communal), editing and adding to them, curates a library of landscape, to build on and anchor us, wherever we go. If it includes the wild world in its sense of reciprocity and belonging (wherever you are from) then the place, the memory and touchstone continues to live, even though it may change.

Community like this is an awareness that we are all involved, all have a stake, are responsible, implicated, invested and interested. It is mutually supportive, seeking to understand and sometimes, yes of course, to compromise. Nature belongs to the land as we all do, but doesn't recognise boundaries, or ownership – much like the wild clematis or bedwine that weaves through the hedgerow corridors, seeding, growing, blooming where it is able and showing us, with the warm and friendly lights of its hedge-feathered globes, the ways we can go. In this way, we can ask a farmer not to mow field margins in spring, when we have heard a woodlark singing above them, indicating a nest below: or praise and thank them for not flail-cutting a winter berry-laden hedge this time round.

Responsibility or stewardship for nature doesn't therefore lie just with the landowner. That's a heavy load to bear (or not bear) and must be shared among us all, one way or another, if we are to stem the catastrophic loss of it and stop cutting off the branch we are sitting on.

So can it be that boundary-less nature invites these crossovers of responsibility and engagement between landowner or farmer and everyone else, if it is considered part of the community? Absolutely. Our farmland birds are a great example. The lapwing – the green plover, peewit, teuchat – a bird with as many surviving names as wild clematis, is a favourite and classic example, a motif of rural community. In southern England we are losing them as breeding birds. To older generations in the village, the lapwings' looping, bubbling call of excitement meant spring. Once perfectly evolved and attuned to our farming practices, lapwings are now destroyed by them. In a generation, they have gone from being white-smocked field familiars to being unrecognised by villagers and farmers alike.

They stopped being part of our story and, ergo, part of our landscape and lives. After ten years of absence, two pairs turned up in a farmer's field next to us: a sudden spin of spread wings, wider at the tip like the tines on a hay tedder; 'hands' outsized at the ends, like goalkeeper's gloves. A wobble, a swoop and the wuthering wheeze of wings through the air and I am transported, my heart in my mouth. But I know these are almost-ghosts. This is a slight-return only; an ebbing of an endling. A local extinction where there used to be thousands.

I messaged the farmer, publicly, warmly, on Facebook, galvanising others and pinpointing the birds, between the pub and the farm: appealing to the farmer's sense of pride in his yeomanship. He didn't know about lapwings, but wanted to help. He delayed ploughing and let me mark the nest until four chicks hatched, up and running like foals straight away: flint-and-chalk pom-poms, ducking behind clods when corvid shadows threatened, until they went into the paddock of a new neighbour. Charmed by his fluffy new tenants and the elegant, acrobatic diligence of the parents, the new neighbour agreed readily to delay cutting his own field, read up about them, took beautiful photos and shared those on Facebook. A circle of protection, concern and delight was formed around these avian celebrities.

Sometimes, it feels like we are trying to save the very last of species, because we are. And that includes ourselves. The connections those birds made us, from a light trespass of spotting them, brought the farmer (oft-beleaguered by public opinion and misunderstanding) and villagers, on-the-lead dog walkers and a new neighbour into the fold, with a new story, greater awareness from all, and let's face it, a warm, tuzzy-muzzy feeling. A community widens.

Boundary-crossing birds invite us to engage in our communities, for the common good. They are noticeable, delightful, vulnerable. And, of course, this isn't just restricted to 'the countryside'. Blackbirds, robins and wrens, ostensibly woodland dwellers, show us how our towns and cities, industrial estates and retail parks can be woodlands, too. If we plant (and keep!) trees and manage areas for wildlife, that is better for us all. A thrush nesting in the cup of an amber traffic light and posted on social media shows how willing we are to embrace, accommodate and celebrate nature in our midst, as part of our daily commute and community anywhere: get ready, go!

My small town of Hungerford is a far friendlier environment for hedgehogs to live than the chemically soaked, slug-pelleted, strimmed, flailed and mown hedgerows and fields of this rural landscape. With holes punched through garden fences, they can travel across boundaries, meet and feed and are loved by their human neighbours. The town is also becoming one of a growing number of 'Swift Towns'. Swifts are extraordinary birds, that only touch the earth when they've found a building to nest in and can spend years in the air. They make exciting, fairground-screaming, Wurlitzer-flights above our high street, schools, churches, common and water meadows. They are thrilling, fascinating, but fast diminishing, because they share our buildings and insect-raising spaces, and we've forgotten that. Or never acknowledged the importance of that. So now we cheer and marvel at them, find out about them, love them and, before we know it, have the beginnings of saving them, because they have been coming to *our* town, all the way from Africa each year, since it was built (and it's a very old town). Swifts are gateway birds to community. Chemicals are dispensed with, wildflowers left to grow, geography lessons created around them, poems read and written, and nestboxes built in workshops. Everybody wins in a Swift Town, and their reach extends beyond twinning towns, to a global community of care.

I worked for The Conservation Volunteers (TCV) in the late nineties, whose ethos is 'connecting people and green spaces to deliver lasting outcomes for both'. The charity has been around for sixty-five years. One of many community and nature

initiatives they have pioneered is the 'Green Gym', founded with 'social prescribing' legend Dr William Bird of Sonning Common, Berkshire, when I was working there. It was, still is, revolutionary, and harks back to that idea of community 'barn-raising'. People working together in a green space for nature, coppicing, scything, planting, wilding, in parks and nature reserves, for physical, mental, societal and environmental health reasons – the common good, on any land that needs it.

Local need and knowledge is key, but doesn't have to have anything to do with where you are from. It's to do with how you engage and how you are welcomed, and we all have an important part to play in that. Being an inquisitive, sensitive 'nosy neighbour' plays a big role. A role that gently challenges and enquires, supports and gets to know its human and wild inhabitants; their names, what they need, if they are OK. Community is a desire to find out: a responsibility to, a vigilance. If you'd not heard from a neighbour in a while, you'd knock – and that applies to wildlife, too. You go out and look for it, you check in, bear witness and raise the alarm if you need to. It's bothering, and bothering to act for your closest neighbours, because in the specific is the universal, and specificity gives you access.

We need an urgent shift in our relationship with nature that can only come with access, action and care. It is in the community of nature and togetherness that we find our sense of belonging and connection − of being home. A commonty of service and joy.

THE ARCHITECTURE OF BELONGING

CAIRN

Although cairns have been built throughout human history, although they have been found across almost every terrain of the world, in today's hyper-politicised countryside they have become yet another trip-hazard of partisan debate.

But cairns, from the Gaelic word for a 'heap of stones', are not one thing. They have been used across history for a variety of purposes: the Vikings employed them as lighthouses, creating stacks of rock on coastlines to jut out from the misty horizon, and this tradition of stacks of stones as waymarkers continues today, used by American trail builders in National Parks, allowing people to identify less popular, less obvious routes, following them like a trail of breadcrumbs. Many cultures, such as those in Peru and Mongolia, used them to mark burial sites, and, as such, many across the globe have turned into sites of ceremony and ritual. Like the shrines to the Virgin Mary seen on routes through Catholic cultures, they are imbued with social-spiritual customs and meanings, but unlike their figurative Catholic iterations, they give no outward indication as to their precise meaning. Cairns are faceless totems to a receded divinity.

The most common type of cairn in the British Isles is the pile of stones at the top of the mountain, an accumulation of individual pebbles brought up by countless hikers. This tradition has been linked to an old Highland custom where each warrior would place a stone on a pile before heading out to battle. Those who survived the slaughter returned home and removed a stone from the heap. The pile of stones that remained was a visual tally of the lives lost in battle, each pebble a palm-sized tombstone for each life lost. This heap of stones would then form the basis of the memorial to these warriors, and the battle itself, building a waymarker of human history onto the land. This custom is the probable source of the Scottish Gaelic blessing: *cuiridh mi clach air do chàrn*, meaning 'I'll put a stone on your stone'. Seen in this light, cairns become a visual manifestation of solidarity, throwing your life on the line for your brothers and sisters.

Today mountain cairns are echoes of this tradition, and they express a solidarity not between clans but between strangers. These days the cairn is a visual expression not of lives lost, but a celebration of lives being lived, a communal monument to the heart-thumping, thigh-straining effort to achieve the view from the top of the mountain. The cairn, a statue made of stones, is actually a static midpoint in a never-ending process, a deeply poetic expression of our ongoing emotional entanglement with the outside world.

But then social media came along. As is not uncommon when consumer culture takes hold of an ancient folk custom, Instagram took all the depth of a multidimensional tradition and flattened it into a square photo, a simulacrum of meaning whose value is measured in the currency of accumulated digital hearts. The hashtag 'stonestacking' is related to cairns only in terms of the material and mechanics. Across the world, across time, people have stacked stones not to create a symbol, but for the process, for the sheer meditative concentration it requires to balance a rock in an improbable position on a pile of others. They make for beautiful photos, a freeze frame of tension, seemingly defying gravity, but the algorithm of social media has encouraged a proliferation of the art, to the point that those in charge of our National Parks, and concerned with the health of its habitats, are clamping down on the practice.

It was when Zion National Park in Utah posted on Facebook two photos of a protected area, one containing several stacks of stones, and one after these stacks had been removed, that the farrago began. The photos were accompanied by text which made the authority's perspective clear: 'stacking up stones is simply vandalism'. As with graffiti, beauty is not in the eye of the beholder, but the lease holder. The thousand or so comments that followed, a standard slosh of outraged vitriol from either side, was just the start of it.

The arguments against stone stacking range from fairly robust ecological concerns to ideologies deeply revealing of the nature of our relationship with the natural world. Stones and rocks can actually be the host to micro-habitats, worlds and processes too small to be of concern to a recreational tourist. To disturb them can disturb the homes and patterns of insects, reptiles and small mammals, and dislodge plants and soil, which can lead to rainfall erosion. On many of the more wayward paths, stacks of stones are sometimes vital waymarkers, and the introduction of new stacks outside of the logic of a route can cause confusion; though the number of times this is problematic is near negligible, the impact of just one instance can be serious, and potentially fatal. But those comments do not form the lion's share of the complaints. By far the most prominent concern is how these human footprints defile the pristine purity of the wilderness.

So deep in our European consciousness is John Muir's misguided vision of the Californian wilderness as a place untouched by man that human presence in nature is synonymous with a defilement of the wild. So ingrained is this fable that it has led to a kind of conceptual myopia in the countryside. Tourists in the British uplands are able to walk past hundreds of acres of sheep-wrecked meadows to say that it was a shame to see a cairn on the way. Quoted in the *New Yorker*, one cairn-removal volunteer from Orkney said: 'It struck me as a real shame, because there are very few places where you can still find solitude and seclusion, and here they were absolutely covered by the footprint of man.' To weed out this deep-set shame of human presence in nature is to see cairns again in their original light: they are monuments to the need each of us has for solitude and seclusion, a need that is part of a long emotional heritage shared by our ancestors. A cairn is more than just a sign that says 'I was here'; it is a testament to remind us that being here, in the wild open spaces, is intrinsic to being human.

8

Culture

NICK HAYES, RIVER THAMES

The answer to the question 'what is to become of England?'
will not be found in the plastic soundbites of today's tem-
plate politicians. It will not emerge from the black and white
lines of traditional print journalism, nor the binary coding of
discourse on social media. To find a way out of this labyrinth of
right or left, to emerge from this underground car park into what
remains of our natural world, we must turn instead to a scarecrow with a robin for a heart and a turnip for a head: Worzel
Gummidge.

First aired in 2019, Mackenzie Crook's remake of a series of
books first published in the 1930s pretends to be a children's
programme. Two foster kids come for a short stay in the countryside, and it's only when a scarecrow in the middle of a field
accidentally breaks the first rule of scarecrowing (don't talk
to the humans) that the door to a magical secret is opened to
them: in the countryside, everything is alive.

The series is steeped in folk culture, from the theme which
Northumbrian band The Unthanks magpied from the Cotswold
Morris tune 'Princess Royal', to Michael Palin's Green Man
and Vanessa Redgrave's Old Mother Carey. It evokes a dreamtime of English culture, where children can speak to animals,
where handcrafted figurines come alive the moment the humans

turn their backs, where the world tree Yggdrasil lies forgotten, snagged with plastic bags, in a supermarket car park.

In the first episode, it's harvest time, but the corn won't ripen. Worzel has to remember how to find the key to unlock the seasons, and with the help of his two human friends, and a brief alliance with his sworn enemies the crows, they gather the local scarecrows together. Earthy Mangold, an allotment scarecrow and mother figure to the rabble, sets them off on a rhyme, a rhyme which turns into a rhythm, which leads them into a dance, which creates printed patterns and signs in the corn, which unlocks the turn of the seasons. The next day, the corn has ripened, apples fall from the trees, autumn has appeared overnight; words, song and dance have changed the nature of reality. Somebody call the ombudsman, this is more than children's telly: smuggled into our living rooms, this is point-blank paganism.

If this was Roman Britain, the Praetorian Guard would already be on to it. Any mention of Worzel Gummidge or Saucy Nancy would be banned, Mackenzie Crook's wattle-and-daub home would be billowing with smoke and he would be hiding deep in the greenwoods, fed by an underground network of dissident BBC executives. But, with the great success of the show, no one seems to have cottoned on. Crook is in the clear, he shares a home in North London with his family and an almost tame robin called Winter George, and a land-based spirituality is seeping into our culture once again.

The insurgency is everywhere. The hashtag #witch on TikTok has 24.1 billion views and over 19 million on Instagram. The autonomy, pluralism, diversity and creativity of pagan philosophies chimes with the re-empowerment of the queer and feminist movements of our time. The all-female Morris side Boss Morris recently appeared on the BRIT Awards, flicking hankies to a live rendition of 'Chaise Longue' by Wet Leg. With the Pig Dyke Molly dancers from the Fens dressed like

Tim Burton extras, with the Beltane and Black Swan Border dancers manifesting a ragged folk horror aesthetic, with the 'obby 'osses, therianthropic beasties of owl masks, stags, goats and green men, a younger generation has assertively snatched Morris from the starched shirts and stiff knees of its fringe practitioners and made it their own. One of the Boss Morris side who appeared at the BRITs, Rhia Davenport, runs a not-for-profit shop and venue in Stroud called Weven, the Nordic word for web. The place is a hub for traditional and contemporary craft makers, and seeks to revive many of the crafts on the red list of the Heritage Craft Association, in other words, those due for imminent extinction. And as such, the shop is something of a witch's cottage – a nexus in a web of relations, that keeps the old ways alive. Speaking on a new online platform for traditional arts, Tradfolk.co, Rhia situates this surge of folk culture in a renewed relationship with the land: 'the folk scene has been having this huge resurgence for the last few years. It's not just the music. The landscape revival has also been happening. It's sort of a spiritual folk revival, I suppose.'[1]

And as Worzel on the BBC has demonstrated, this landscape spiritualist revival is moving in from the margins and generating a cultural renaissance at the heart of society. The book *The Lost Words*, illustrated by Jackie Morris, a project that sought to restore and honour some of the nature words lost in the *Oxford Junior Dictionary*, was shortlisted as one of Britain's favourite nature books of all time. It was so successful it spawned a musical version, *Spell Songs*, which is onto its second album. The theatre director and actor Simon McBurney's adaptation of Susan Cooper's folk horror *The Dark Is Rising* was recently broadcast on BBC Radio 4, and the musician Johnny Flynn's album, *Lost in the Cedar Wood*, saw the 4,000-year-old *Epic of Gilgamesh*, the story of a magical forest and its destruction, rebirthed for twenty-first-century Britain. The magus at the heart of all three projects, Robert Macfarlane, is due to publish a book on how 'rivers, forests and mountains are living beings'. The old ways have returned, magicke is mainstream; it won't be long before Fiona Bruce is casting runes on the six o'clock news.

The Lost Words sparked a fuse across the country. *Spell Songs* have been embraced across party lines, extolled by the *Telegraph* and *Guardian* alike; there is something in them that speaks to us all. But it's how these artists describe their purpose that should give authorities most concern. The website claims these songs are 'a chance to sing nature back to life'[2] and describes them as 'spells or incantations, where art *conjures* nature'. This is the old Hebrew and Aramaic magic of Abracadabra, meaning 'I will create as I speak' and the idea that art can change reality, that it is possible to sing nature back to life, places *Spell Songs* much closer to shamanism than the entertainment industry. The origin of the word 'conjure' is also another clue to this new direction of English culture. Conjure means in this context 'to bring to mind', but in the Middle Ages it meant 'to summon by a sacred name, invoke by incantation or magic', branching from the Latin meaning to swear an oath, or to conspire. Rather than seeing nature as simply the muse, the object of an artist's imagination, culture is re-entering a kinship with nature, collaborating with it.

And it's not just the arts. In that other great storytelling tradition, the law, concepts such as ecocide are gaining traction, aiming to reassess processes such as industrial fishing, oil spillage, mining, deforestation and other extractive actions upon which our modern world is based as the murder of ecologies, with an appropriate legal response. With organisations such as Lawyers for Nature conspiring to bring nature rights in and of itself, the law is beginning to recognise trees and rivers as more than just commodities. Following examples set in countries such as India and New Zealand, this is an emancipation from anthropocentric definitions of nature as property or resource; instead, nature has 'personhood' and represented by people it can launch legal cases against those who try to harm it. Amazing Grace: it is as if the great galleon of supremacist capitalist rationalism is finally changing course, and heading back to a land of *animism*.

For much of the last two centuries, animism has been a catch-all term to describe the innumerable cultural philosophies that existed before organised religion, the understanding that the land had a soul, that rivers, trees, stones, even works of art possessed a spirit that humans considered worthy of worship. The word was not given to us by animist cultures, the First Nations that practise its beliefs to this day, but superimposed by European projections. The man who popularised the word, Edward Tyler, considered animism a primitive stage of human evolution, which developed into organised religion, and which, in turn, would be abandoned for the ultimate comprehensive grip on the world, scientific rationality.

But a more modern reading of animist cultures has recently developed, seeing this focus on the soul of non-human objects as a preoccupation of the Christian mindset. What forms the fabric of the animist worldview is in fact the relationships between entities, the reciprocal flow of energy, the exchange of gifts. As Graham Harvey writes in the second edition of his book *Animism: Respecting the Living World*: 'questions about what defines life (e.g. the possession of souls, spirits, minds, intentionality or agency) have been replaced by questions about what behaviours constitute respect when persons of different species interact.'

With this new trend towards animist thought patterns, the culture of this land is finally beginning to answer the Anthropocene. And the Praetorian Guard of neoliberalism had better act quickly and shut this whole fandango down, because none of its orthodoxies are safe any more. In an interview about the release of his album with Johnny Flynn, Rob

Macfarlane said, 'to me, a forest is a living entity — a complex super organism with a glorious intricacy and consciousness unto itself. Watching [Enkidu and Gilgamesh] strip Humbaba of seven auras — to me, there's almost no more powerful, resonant parable of what we have done. We have systematically stripped the world of its auras in order to convert it into a resource.'[3] What will become of the government's road-building programme if the voters suddenly wake up to this way of thinking, to the language of auras over spreadsheets, to parables over pledges? If rivers are considered to have personhood, not just by the law, but by the locals who take it upon themselves to act as their guardians, how will water companies across the globe be able to afford the legal costs of using them as sewerage? If our culture concentrates on the relationships between communities and nature, rather than the simplistic legal fiction of owner and property, what will happen to the brick walls and barbed wire fences that block us from kinship? As feminist scholar Val Plumwood writes of the modern animist movement, 'The first [necessary task] is to re-situate the human in ecological terms, and the second is to re-situate the nonhuman in ethical terms.' If this happens, then everything from big oil to deep-sea dredging, factory farms, chemical pesticides, plastic production, exclusionary fences, the whole lot, every human practice that harms ecologies will become crimes against nature, and (because a line no longer exists between the two) its communities. The system doesn't so much crash, it melts into air.

So it's no wonder that activists are calling on the power of myth, the stories that animate our landscape. In early 2023, when the High Court ruled that a centuries-long tradition of wild camping on Dartmoor was to be extinguished because a hedge-fund manager wanted to assert his right of total dominion over 4,000 acres of it, activists responded by invoking a local spirit of the moors, Old Crockern. They made a giant puppet of the creature, dressed it in rags and led a musical procession of 3,500 people across Dartmoor. While the Dartmoor National Park Authority wrangled in court with the hedge-fund manager's lawyers, arguing over the legal parameters of the word *recreation*, local activists decided that instead of repeatedly pushing at the Overton window, they would pass through its panes like a wraith. They responded in myth. By raising Old Crockern, they were reigniting an ancient code of custom with the land, one of reciprocity and sustainability that had existed long before laws were created to legitimise their exclusion. By refusing the legal limits imposed upon our experience of nature they were fighting the logos of land law with the mythos of folklore.

Logos and mythos are two nebulous concepts, hard to define on their own and better understood in their relationship. Seen in terms of land, logos is the advance of monocultural ideology, a top-down superstructure enforced onto societies that has justified for centuries the extractions of minerals, the ploughing of meadows and the exclusion of our communities. The seed of the logos of our land is that original greenwash word used by Tudors, Georgians and Victorians to justify the enclosure and exploitation of resources: *improvement*. Improvement is a term used by philosophers, speculators and jurists, from the 1500s to this very day, to describe the idea that if you can turn a piece of land to profit, you have justified your total dominion of it. This unquestioned creed that framed nature as a resource for human extraction became the deepest orthodoxy at the heart of English land ownership and the countryside we see today is an extrapolation of its logic.

Mythos, on the other hand, is what has to be destroyed for logos to claim dominion: it is a shared, localised understanding of the land, its ecology and the community that cares for it. Mythos is the mesh of traditions that arose from the landscape as expressions of the experience of place, stories and songs and customs that kept people in relationship with nature, foregrounded its importance to our lives, reminded us what we owed it. This culture is much older than the laws of England, and much older than any notion of England itself. In land, logos is the command of exclusive ownership, mythos the song of collective belonging.

And logos is winning, because logos has all the money and, in the following cases, all the gumption. In April 2022, when the government suppressed a report that they themselves had commissioned, which had recommended a 'quantum shift in how our society supports people to access and engage with the outdoors',[4] there was an angry response from the access community. A government minister, Mark Spencer, was shoved in front of the microphones to respond, and, with the usual nod to our much-lauded English right to walk in straight lines past nature (our Rights of Way network) he explained simply that 'the English countryside is a place of business'. Six months earlier, John Leyland, the Environment Agency's chief of staff, was thrown in front of a bus full of journalists to explain why water companies had dumped raw sewage into the rivers and seas of England more than 400,000 times in 2021. What if people got ill by swimming? Instead of acknowledging the health risks posed by these overflows, he replied, 'The rivers that we have are not there for human swimming.'[5] These two statements are cracks in the Apollonian mask of the English countryside that show just how mad it is. The logos is so wrapped up in its own logic that it actively ignores tens of thousands of years of human entanglement with nature in favour of the last 200 years of its industrialisation. Logos needs you to believe that business interests supersede all other relationships with nature and that the 'purpose' of rivers is to accommodate chemical and human waste. With all its money and its powerful systems of normalisation, logos will keep shouting until the last tree is grubbed out, until the rivers run to sludge and only when the birds have ceased to sing will it too run out of breath.

Mythos, the storying of the landscape, the ritualistic expression of our social bond with nature, is our only hope. But much harm has been done to the English mythos. Hugh Lupton, one of our foremost oral storytellers, writes in his book *The Dreaming of Place*: 'I'm not making any great claims for English oral tradition. It has been badly damaged by our history – the enclosures, the industrial revolution, early mass literacy, the breakdown of community. It is scattered and fragmented.' Enclosure is often described in terms of economics, but rarely are its impacts on culture considered. The crime of enclosure was not only our exclusion from the countryside, nor was it just the accumulation of private capital via dispossession of public wealth, but it was also the dissolution of our cultural relationship with the land. When the use of land is directed not by the community that lives on it, but by one individual owner, a monoculture of ideology holds total dominion. As the forests are cleared for the plough, so too are the stories that tell of our relationships with the forest; ecocide begets mythocide. Seasonal festivities are banned, heritage crafts die out, it becomes pointless, or twee, to tell the stories of the land that we have no contact with. Instead of the rich diversity of expression that came with an autonomous experience of nature, our interaction with the outside world is filtered through the banal corporate construction of the leisure industry. The temple of Pan has become an Airbnb listing. But just as weeds creep through the concrete, so Lupton is positive about our cultural tradition with the land: 'it is still there, waiting to be reassembled and retold, to be transformed from the secret depths of silence into articulate speech and song – and it's ours … it is the dreaming of these particular landscapes.'

But there, in those last words, is the central complication to England's animist revival. So much damage has been done to our culture, through years of exclusion from the land, that we can only bridge the gap with the mythopoetic paradigms of other cultures. And those cultures are the very same cultures we very nearly eradicated through imposing the logos of *improvement* onto other lands. Cultural genocide was a key tactic of colonialism: to exploit the resources of other countries, the mechanics of European imperialism had to destroy the relationships that communities held with the land. From Ireland to Canada, from Australia to the Caribbean, native language, art, song and dance were all recognised as cultural practices that bonded communities with each other and with their land, and all, at some point, were banned. Culture became synonymous with civilisation, urbanisation, with the sophistication of the European enlightenment, while nature was understood as wild, barbaric, uncultivated, a raw material in need of improvement. Culture, once seen as our connective tissue to the non-human, became fenced off from nature and it, too, was enclosed in institutions: museums, galleries, Netflix, temples of civilisation. By imposing this ideology on other lands, we cemented it deeper into ours.

The title of Lupton's book, *The Dreaming of Place*, derives from an Australian Aboriginal concept, 'the Dreaming', a mindscape of stories that dates back some 65,000 years. The Dreaming is understood by Aboriginal people as 'a beginning that never ended',[6] a world of spirits, gods and ancestors, human and non-human, that are both long gone and living in current time, in a parallel universe on earth. It is a mythological construct that informs how humans interact with the living world, an invisible magnetic field generated between Aboriginal communities and their landscape, that sets the moral compass of their societies. It is not dissimilar to the Irish conception of Tír na nÓg, the otherworld of Celtic mythology, or Annwn, its Welsh expression, and the faintest trace of it can still be seen in the English celebration of Samhain, when the veil between this world and the world of spirits is said to be at its thinnest. But to rely on this great tapestry in order to reweave the remaining threads of our culture of the land is to ignore that we once tried to tear it to pieces. The Dreamtime of Aboriginal culture suffered relentless vandalism by imperialist drive of 'assimilation', the blind need to Europeanise indigenous cultures, retrain their minds to the same logos imposed on English minds centuries before. Reservations, state laws, the abduction of between 25,000 and 100,000 mixed-race children from their Aboriginal homes drove a rabbit-proof fence between the elders and their younger generations, cutting the xylem that allowed the root culture to feed its branches. Dreamtime survived, but no thanks

to us. Without first acknowledging the harm we did to other cultures we cannot begin to address the damage done to ours.

To reconstruct our connection to land we have to resurrect our connection to myth. We must use our imagination, the wildest creature in the menagerie of our minds, to conspire with nature. We must tell stories, old and new, that regenerate a culture of mythos that exposes logos for the madness that it is. And Worzel is no bad place to start. If England is the ten-acre field of Worzel Gummidge, then its people are the two protagonists, orphaned children searching for a home in nature. And the scarecrow, a turnip in a hat, is the imaginative collusion between nature and man, the bridge between our experience and that of the living world; he is the imaginative leap that bridges the human and the non-human and creates connection. It is easy to dismiss Worzel Gummidge as make-believe. But this, too, is a symptom of logos. Because the root of the word make-believe could well be the source of our new mythos, the first step to regenerating a culture of care. From the Germanic *lieben*, to make-believe is to make beloved.

WILD SERVICE IN ACTION

PAUL'S WILD BEE SANCTUARY

Paul is @the_beeguy on Twitter (X). His wife is @The_BeeGirl. From what he says on the phone, his kids are the bee kids, though they're too young for Twitter right now. The family lives and breathes bees, and together they run the world's only wild bee sanctuary, in the foothills of the Wicklow Mountains, in Co. Wicklow, Ireland.

Every day, Paul and his wife post photos and videos from their sanctuary, and bitesize bee facts drawn from the dense PhD papers and science journals they review in their evenings. He estimates he spends four to five hours a day on the admin, raising funds for his bee sanctuary and raising awareness for bees across Ireland. The website he curates makes clear their goals: 'to educate, to advocate, to take action and to disrupt'. As the site says: 'we need to ensure that people know about bees, understand their plight, the causes and consequences of their declining numbers and the solutions that are available.' Bee stats are horrific, and the problem is that no one engages with them. Forty per cent of bees worldwide are now vulnerable to extinction. This is part of a wider decline in insect species across Europe – between 1991 and 2018 the populations of our flying insects have decreased by 76 per cent. Scientists predict a complete collapse of insect populations, and the beginning of a landslide catastrophe for the rest of the world's ecosystems within ten years.

Paul has no training; he is not an entomologist, biologist, botanist, or any kind of scientist. He grew up in the Dublin suburbs and quit college to play bass in a rock band. He cites another band with brothers as frontmen, Oasis, as an indication of the dynamics that led to the band breaking up and why he ended up doing odd jobs, landscape gardening, dry stone walling, manual labour and so on to keep up with the rent. He and his wife, a veterinary nurse at the time, were looking to move out of Wexford, looking for cheap farmland around Ireland to bring up their kids. They found a bit of land, fifty-five acres in total, that a farmer had sold to a group planning to develop it into a shooting business. They had planted lots of trees, and left the bramble and spurge as cover for the pheasant. It never developed into anything, and so when Paul and his wife bought it they had planned to plough up the earth, clear the bramble and make a market garden selling salads. But since the deer and rabbits had it all in the first year, and he couldn't afford a deer fence, they had to change tack. Rather than imposing his own plans onto the land, maybe it was easier to follow nature. Sitting there hearing the buzz of the bees like a loud roar, he realised that he was already in a bee sanctuary, and that he should devote his life to protecting and promoting it.

His sanctuary is a mess of nature. From his website: 'We are fields of wildflower meadows, sunflowers, phacelia, clovers and mustard buzzing with bees and dancing with butterflies; we are vast hedgerows unkempt and full of nettles, brambles, thistles, wildflowers and life. We are trees filled with a cacophony of birdsong.' By letting his fifty-five acres grow, wild and untamed, by resisting the urge towards neatness, or rat poison, he has created a perfect haven for bees. And because bees are keystone species, that habitat is perfect for so much more. He has swifts in his toilet. The barn owl box they installed some years ago was occupied within five days. His sanctuary is des res for wildlife.

Paul's primary mission is, as he puts it, to 'correct the narrative'. This narrative stems from a deep anthropocentric orthodoxy woven into our understanding of bees: honey. Of the ninety-nine species of bee in Ireland, only one bee produces honey. There are twenty-one species of bumble bee and the remaining seventy-seven species are known as solitary bees, which provide the vital service of pollination, but whose contribution goes unsung by the media and wildlife organisations tasked with protecting them. Solitary bees are generally smaller than honeybees and have an extraordinary variety of colour and shape. Most of their short lives are spent within their nest, usually burrowed by the females into the soil, and they are only active for a few weeks between spring and autumn. The work they do during that time forms almost 80 per cent of their estimated value to the Irish economy: 53 million euros.

Paul learned about bees on the job. He learned about habitat restoration by watching it grow. By being totally immersed in this sanctuary, he learned about nature the old way, through patient observation. He has a huge respect for science but feels it is lacking the creative communications skills needed to really reach out and touch people. He takes the video footage, and his wife, a keen portrait photographer, takes the close-up photos of the bees they feature. His job is to bring the sanctuary to tens of thousands of people across the globe, steadily eroding the cartoon image of the honeybee, and replacing it with the complex diversity of what is being lost.

The popularity of his Twitter (X) feed, and the unique nature of his sanctuary, have brought him into contact, and sometimes conflict, with organisations that hold power. This is where his fourth goal, disruption, comes into play. The most prominent threat to bees is the way we produce food, the way we remove habitat for industrial farming, the way we spray chemicals on an industrial scale. You can buy bee-friendly flowers from a garden centre, but most of those have already been sprayed by pesticides before they enter the garden shop, although no one is saying so.

So *he* says so. By simply owning a piece of land, and living in it with his family, he has no political ties, no funding bodies to hamstring his actions or gag what he says. In his words: 'we can be a bit rock 'n' roll about it.' He sees the deference inherent in the hierarchies of power, the fear of saying something out of place to a government minister, or to a CEO of a wildlife organisation; he sees a code of omerta among the professionals that keeps things unsaid, a code that stalls meaningful change. By just being there, by being vocal, Paul's sanctuary provides an alternative approach that makes it hard for organisations to pretend they have it all under control. He acknowledges the well-meaning attempts of people in organisations, but he feels the conservation sector lacks the urgency of action required to meet the threats to our environment. His website caustically defines the word *now*: 'present time, not soon, not sometime convenient in the future, not after the next conference. Present time.'

9

Education

EMMA LINFORD, CAMBRIDGESHIRE

'All through our youth and adolescence, before the conscious and critical mind begins to act as a sort of censor and guardian at the threshold, ideas seep into our mind, vast hosts and multitudes of them. These years, one might say, our Dark Ages during which we are nothing but inheritors'
— E. F. Schumacher

'The great purpose of school can be realised better in dark, airless, ugly places ... it is to master the physical self, to transcend the beauty of nature. School should develop the power to withdraw from the external world'
— William Tovey Harris

If life is a journey, then Western capitalism touts it as a straight line, soaring upwards — 'a smooth superhighway on which we progress with great speed, but at its end lies disaster,' Rachel Carson prophesied back in 1962. This journey surreptitiously whispers 'keep going, don't stop, you'll get there', wherever there is — the obscurity of self-actualisation, enlightenment, retirement, the end of the rainbow? This is the path of capitalist growth, a blinkered straight line of performative status-bagging bounties heading for an arcane destination. Binding us trance-like is our human need to belong which modernity uses to shame us into thinking that veering off that line would be to malfunction.

Bounded by walls and concrete, the majority of us live a life of domestication, an optimised-for-convenience lifestyle of perceived certainty, that, as philosopher Alain de Botton says, 'keeps us tethered to the person we are in ordinary life who may not be who we essentially are'. Our identities have been possessed by a citizen-consumer ideology which cares only for itself and plunders what it can. Dr Michael Cohen, an American pathologist and geneticist, suggests that humans have the potential for fifty-three senses and suggests that these have atrophied through under-use. This loss of relationship to ourselves, then, is likely to be the result of the disconnection from our own sentient bodies, consequently removing us from our own conscious interconnection in the web of life. Without this interrelatedness we have become 'exhabitants' of our planet, a floating constellation of straitjacketed identities, adrift in a physiological, psychological and spiritual crisis.

Education has played a critical part in influencing this crisis, but it can also lead us out of it. The word education itself has evolved from 'educare', meaning to allow for the human growth of innate gifts and relational potential. Yet mainstream pedagogy continues to mechanise humans for productive growth, ensuring roles are filled to sustain functioning markets − learning reduced to transmissive knowledge, giving and receiving within isolationist subject areas − where learners are receptor vessels, memorising and repeating information, and teachers are 'providers' in a reductive, transactional exchange. Intellect is revered over intelligence, the mind over the body. It's delusional to think that this robotic approach equips us for the task of a lifelong journey to maturity. Education, then, needs to be reimagined as the essential adventure of our time, one that takes the path less travelled towards a 'life-sustaining civilisation', where humans care beyond themselves.

To move a shackled humanity from its supremacist position in the web of life and to cease viewing nature as a resource, I propose an education revolution; a radical reimagining that requires us to take our seats next to and with every other planetary organism. And why not? For we, humanity, constitute the same elements as every other organism on this planet. To become a part of, rather than apart from, this complex planetary ecological system requires a shift in collective consciousness that, crucially, allows for difference, complexity and a spectrum in which there is no hierarchical relational power.

Donna Haraway, professor emerita in the history of consciousness at the University of California, Santa Cruz, encourages us in this ecological crisis to use 'queer' as a verb to disrupt all normative societal sorting operations. So binaries such as them/us, human/nature, female/male, mind/body, wild/civilised will no longer be singular but diverse constellations. Queering therefore mimics the myriad assemblages in a flourishing ecosystem that would otherwise be vulnerable to collapse. It's precisely this addition of diverse proximities that can regenerate our monocropped and undynamic relationships. This regenerative system is adaptive, folding and refolding in an energetic co-evolutionary dance working with uncertainty to foster emergence.

Currently, education robs us of the multiplicity of our being, leaving us unable to relate to the otherness of others, including nature. What kinds of stories can we tell, and what might our relationships with the natural world look like if we allowed ourselves to feel into our whole sentient body and touch our sorrow at the disappearance of our earthly kin? So, at this time in history there are no other important binaries to queer in healing relationships than human/other-than-human, us/them and mind/body. Regenerating these core relational positions will bring us back to a position of care, and I believe the inspiration for this learning needs to come from outdoor education that currently sits at the periphery of our education system.

I've been attempting to disrupt that straight line of capitalism, shredding layers of told-ness, since my first school exam. Following mainstream education I became a design creative — the beating heart of consumerism — hoping to satisfy creative expression while sustaining a livelihood. But an existential malady struck very early on. Realising that my creativity was interminably reduced to a design formula to match a budget, and hoping for salvation, I volunteered for a three-month voluntary expedition to Belize. This entailed being part of a community of British volunteers from diverse social backgrounds, who built and survived in temporary camps for up to a month in three challenging environments: jungle, a remote caye (island) and a small border community. Here, while drinking rusty water sterilised with iodine (no long-term effects so far), eating plantain and biscuits brown (military rations to 'fill and block'), coping with the stench of unwashed human exposed to days of tropical heat and humidity, I was exposed to a culture and life which was far more difficult than and different from my own sanitised life. In fact, with these acts of service, facing difficulties together, being resourceful and living on just enough, what I felt was liberation and ultimately a regeneration of who I was, how I related and what I valued. Compared to a culture based on constant striving underpinned by 'it's never enough' neon signage, removing excessive choice and complexity, multitasking to achieve and working with the natural rhythms of the day felt, well, peaceful and meaningful. Yet transferring this metamorphosis back into my society was bewildering and felt like a cruel estrangement from familiar patterns. Society told me that I no longer fitted while an experience told me there were other ways.

The experience had stirred my wild-scape, a palimpsest of body knowledge conjured by distant seas, mountains and jungle, and freed me from a previous conditioned state.

Enlivened by the power of this counter-cultural experience and drawn to social activism, I stepped into an outdoor facilitation role believing that there is no better way to regenerate ourselves and impact community than through the experiences provided by an outdoor environment. Outdoor education comes in many forms, ranging from hard-skill instruction to therapy, soul work, environmental education, adventure education and land working. Despite this broad pedagogy, all forms of outdoor education are commonly united by the encouragement of dynamic experience. This approach offers multiple possibilities in unearthing our inherent capabilities and expanding our relationships to self and other. One pedagogy I'd particularly like to illuminate is that of adventurous learning journeys, or expeditions, as a method of queering the aforementioned binaries. Journeys like these are typically geographically remote, multi-day, outcome-based and provide an inconvenient quality that agitates the everyday. The transformations I've witnessed have been profound. Some speak of being given 'a new chance at life' and 'a feeling of belonging' that they've never experienced before; their posture, behaviour, sense of self, fearlessness in uncertainty and their relationship to others are redesigned. For many, these journeys are a rite of passage that has led them to new directions they thought unnavigable.

Here the straight line shapes itself into an arc, following the mythic structure of Joseph Campbell's *The Hero's Journey*, where the journey maker responds to a call to adventure, participates in challenging experiences and finally incorporates the learned wisdom back into community. These journeys lure us off the line to pull on untried skins and embolden us to step over a threshold of self through challenge and adversity. Placing our tame selves

within an animate ecosystem of elemental forces and geography demands an intimate and constantly reflexive relational muscle. The potential for transformation is as diverse as the alternating conditions; jumbling us around, planing our behavioural edges, provoking a sprinkle of humility here, more patience there.

The inconvenient conditions flatten social hierarchies and force individuals to co-exist and collaborate in mutualistic fashion. The group becomes a co-dependent, resilient, self-regulating ecological system, each organism an agental actor in service to the whole community. Political theorist Emily Beausoleil suggests that to cultivate healthy, caring relationships, one needs to be attentive to the 'pulse' and 'pause' of encounter, where we must privilege the ethics of 'receptivity and responsiveness over pre-given moral codes'. Our entrenched predispositions originate from a culture of blame and uncare and validate inequality and selfishness. These have to be renegotiated with empathic response-ability to benefit the whole simply because being unresponsive in extreme conditions is irresponsible and precipitates uncomfortable consequences for all: exposure, hunger, fatigue, grumpiness! The dynamic and ever-emergent position of participants also requires masterful relational attention and adaptation from the facilitator. Possessing a multitude of skills — mentor, leader, therapist, medic, coach — that must be convened with careful crafting to allow and enable individual flourishing.

Moving through a landscape allows for a daily schedule of forward travel with overnight interludes. As we progress, our thinking minds submerge and our bodies become alive, intuiting, inter- and intra-acting with the topography. Risk and certainty are given alternative reference points. Pausing to wild camp allows time for unravelling and reassembling. It has the potential of a primeval communion with other-than-human kin. The tent skin is a permeable membrane allowing one nature to

animate the other. Being moored in one place invites a quies-
cence, sequestering our attention away from societal complexity
into the small adventures of place. As Nan Shepherd so atten-
tively writes, 'no one knows the [mountain] completely who has
not slept on it. As one slips over into sleep, the mind grows limp;
the body melts; perception alone remains. One neither thinks
nor desires, nor remembers, but dwells in pure intimacy with
the tangible world.' Grounded in listening and witnessing, these
encounters often conjure awe and empathy – awe to accept our
place in interconnected systems and empathy connecting us to
difference.

Yet, despite limitless potential for transforming human
relationships and a promising connection to nature, adventure
education has significant shortcomings, needing timely intervention. Most significant of all is the dominant human-centric
narrative. Journeys are outcome based, typically summit bound,
and chiefly objectify nature. The model, founded by the educator Kurt Hahn around a century ago, was designed to break
down the ego using challenge to overcome limits such as fear.
Fear is a human instinct and by endeavouring to overcome it
we ignore our human wholeness. Yet wouldn't it be more
wholesome to learn to walk with fear rather than attempting
to banish it? Metrics such as grit, coping and mental toughness
are applauded and, though participants generally return with
increased self-esteem and confidence, the learning barely tips its
hat to the environment, and more feminine traits such as vulnerability, compassion and empathy are largely ignored or scoffed
at. Rather than espousing the merits of these gains, isn't it more
fitting to ask why our society demands this of us? Do we need
more education which drives us to ignore our wholeness and
encourages us to strive to be above the ecology of living things?

The natural world doesn't discriminate against social background, age or class, but, due to wealth and privilege, this

human-centric education further broadens socio-economic inequality. The perception of where nature is and where it's most highly valued is also skewed, where wildness is perceived to be 'out there', beyond our urban fences. Interestingly, the concept of 'wild' is itself a social construct, originating from the American frontier which separated civilised society from the perceived barbarity of primitive forest-dwelling humans. And as these more remote experiences are typically singular or at best occasional, they hold little continuity in learning once returning back to familial urban green spaces; the experiences and wisdom learned also become separate and often abandoned. How, then, can we reassemble this regenerative pedagogy so that we also see and feel ourselves as part of an interdependent system, wherever we are located, to feel that we belong and therefore care for it?

I propose introducing an ambitious new philosophy of practice that journeys towards an 'ecological self'. The term and ideology was first coined in 1972 by Arne Naess, a co-founder of the environmental philosophy and social movement known as 'deep ecology'. This journey moves beyond anthropocentrism, locating human concerns with a relational closeness to nature. By consciously allowing the natural world to influence our own evolving identity, an ethic of care towards the other-than-human world is strengthened.

This proposal goes well beyond increasing environmental education into all learning programmes; this is a reimagining of what outdoor education could be. All landscapes and perceived non-places, those places around us such as kerbs, roundabouts and school playgrounds, would be brought into proximity, revealing enchantment in the ordinary. These places actually hold many layered texts which, when deciphered, can carefully open a window into the history of life, deep time, evolutionary shifts, ecosystems, our sentient bodies and the planet. Facilitators would need to remodel themselves into transdisciplinary masters of ecology, geology, natural history, dance, movement and storytelling and, instead of working with familiar language such as 'team-working' and 'leadership', look to ecological systems and other-than-humans for inspiration. This practice also has the potential to be portable. Dropping it into local and remote environments alike will remove the wild/ civilised separation of nature and give learners a sustainable gift of belonging that can be deployed anywhere. For, when we realise we are a part of nature, we can bring outdoor education into any space.

Mediating this change will require a new ecological language that attends to the pulse and pause of encounter. We could look to evolving outdoor pedagogies such as rites of passage, eco therapy, eco psychology and forest schooling for inspiration, as they already use divergent language. However, I believe we also need to envisage a more radical, emotionally entwined practice, one that borrows from post-humanist theory and asks the question 'how do we relate to those who don't speak back?' British anthropologist Tim Ingold argues that our capacity to respond to the world isn't innate but is developed through an 'education of evolving responses within and through the environment'. Like Ingold, American philosopher Jane Bennett suggests that, rather than it being a cognitive process, it's the felt experience that actively stimulates connection. She describes it as 'a shedding of layers to be open to a more radical permeability, where we blur the boundaries between ourselves and other, perhaps wanting to know what trees are feeling or wanting to know what they know'.

To answer the question of how we relate to the other through feeling, we must turn to awe and empathy. Both of these states can be triggered by any one or a combination of storytelling, the multi-sensory feeling body and attention. This is the bridge or universal language which allows us to both understand and feel how we are enmeshed with other beings, elements, forces and objects within dynamic assemblages. When 'ignited' or felt within us, either can move our human-centric position of 'having' to an eco-centric one of 'being-with'. This is the language of belonging. And with continued practice — and it is an intentional practice — this has diversified my own being with all parts of me synchronously pupating towards an ecological self. When I listen to the leaf for its story or feel the spirit of the willow, I feel a part of something bigger than me, that I am part of. That feeling is wholesome.

Empathy, the ability to feel from another's perspective, breaks down feelings of separation, creating a porosity of relatedness, and ultimately leads to strong feelings of the unity of everything. And, like flexing a muscle, empathy can be trained to convert the defensive response of difference to a corporeal softening. Poet and writer Sophie Strand invites us to try 'pouring yourself into the mind of every bird, fly, bumble bee, bindweed, grub you see … slip into the shadow of the sturgeon below the river surface, beginning to feel the chemical prickle that will lead the fish upstream to spawn'.

Awe, which astrophysicist Neil deGrasse Tyson describes as a 'spiritual reaction, where words fail you', can be accessed anywhere providing the language is accessible and effective. After all, isn't the mundane just a vessel that hasn't been brought to life or is out of our habitual range of view? Awe can produce feelings of humility and diminishment of the self, the effects of which can stimulate altruism and generate pro-environmental behaviour. As an example, my most recent awe event was crawling along a tarmacked road in Suffolk with a natural history group, magnifying white blotches mistaken for chewing gum. They turned out to be small, lively forests of lichen, a community of symbionts interacting with the tarmac. Gasp! I was so excited to have discovered a miniature extra-terrestrial population! Calling out to share the discovery, my comrades were equally reverent. From that moment onwards, I have carried a magnifier in my rucksack while guiding – for bringing attention to the unseen, physically and metaphorically, is a necessary facilitation skill.

Naturalist and philosopher Alexander von Humboldt stated: 'When nature is perceived as a web, its vulnerability also becomes obvious. Everything hangs together. If one thread is pulled, the whole tapestry may unravel. In this great chain of cause and effects, no single thing can be considered in isolation.' Reimagining outdoor learning is one isolated thread in this tapestry but what if we were to queer the entirety of Western education? What if we centred this new relational ontology, a queer eco pedagogy into all learning systems, at all stages of life from early years education to therapy and business? These 'curriculums of queerness' would reframe the dominant paradigm of performance and success and move it forward to embrace wholeness and diversity. Wouldn't this have a gargantuan regenerative impact?

By looking to natural systems or indigenous cultures we can also reframe *how* we learn. Aboriginal scholar Tyson Yunkaporta describes learning as a 'winding path' that doesn't take a straight path 'but winds, zig-zags, or goes around'. The educative journey could mimic the information exchange nodes in a mycelial network, sites of knowledge acquisitions rather than a destination in itself. It is a processual way of becoming, without destination or needing to be finished. And being taught less and experiencing more, learners encounter their own knowledge, which allows for their own diverse limits.

The most compelling outcome of these imaginative acts would be the redefinition of the facilitation role to account for a merging of subject areas or disciplines. This interdisciplinary role would prioritise outdoor liveliness that inspires experiential

learning and sense-making and where the 'response-ability' of the teacher would move from hierarchical 'teller' to one of the 'attentive listener', or like the gardener tending a seed.

Education that would profoundly impact our collective consciousness and fledge stewards for the planet would be to introduce a 'National Wild Service' for all young adults from all social backgrounds – a longer-term exposure of being with and on the land. This would give learners a felt and meaningful experience of our reciprocal relationship with the land – how it feels, smells and sounds. The result of which would be more connection and empathy for place and people, a collective responsibility for nature and, ultimately, an influence in political and business decision-making. These placements could take a position in the curriculum or as a secondment post-school-leaving age, and could be supported by a coalition of countryside organisations. It would be encouraged that everyone should take this opportunity, privileged and non-privileged alike, to work with their hands in the soil alongside elders and farmers, hedge-laying, growing, harvesting or restoring rain-forest or peat uplands.

In addition, progressive institutions, such as Schumacher College in Devon, could provide a working blueprint for main-stream postgraduate education. The college works with an ethos of 'head, heart and hands', where students are immersed in a community rhythm of growing, harvesting and cooking while studying.

I am sowing ancient seeds in a barren capitalist soil and the alternative journey I am proposing is a queer one that dissolves ingrained binaries, embraces deviant imaginative politics and celebrates our whole sentient selves. It's time to reach out and accommodate different ways of being and learning. I'd like to envisage a culture where difference is normative, where every-body has the opportunity to access a multitude of landscapes that are brought to life by the magic of multidisciplinary educators on a lifelong, wayfaring, learning journey. So, with courage, I invite each of you to transform your binary line into a pulsing, pausing, shapeshifting, learning journey that co-shapes and co-forms with the earth.

WILD SERVICE IN ACTION

LIZ AND THE REBEL BOTANISTS

'Technically, we're breaking the law,' Liz Richmond tells me. 'Chalking on the pavement is illegal, like fly-posting – even though what we're doing is purely educational.'

Liz is the founder of a group calling themselves the Rebel Botanists, dedicated to inspiring the public with botanical knowledge. I find her a few minutes' walk from Plymouth railway station, crouched over a dandelion-like flower, spelling out its Latin name on the pavement in pink chalk: *Sonchus oleraceus*. Common sowthistle. Later, I look it up: this plant, with its bright yellow flower and jagged-edged leaves, can be eaten as a salad crop, and has been ascribed a variety of medicinal usages by Māori and Native American peoples. I realise, to my shame, that I have sometimes pulled it up as a weed.

No such thing as a weed, reads one chalked slogan on the roadside. 'They've all got their individual names,' says Liz. 'Life springs from the smallest cracks.' Liz set up the Rebel Botanists with friends during the coronavirus lockdowns of 2020.[1] The seed for it was planted in her head after seeing the work of a French botanist to reclaim weeds from being overlooked, by chalking the names of them onto pavements.[2] So Liz applied the idea to her hometown of Plymouth and started using her daily lockdown walks to do 'walk and chalk' botany sessions.

A teacher by trade, Liz works with students to reconnect them to nature, embedding biodiversity themes within her art and English courses; she has the bountiful energy and enthusiasm of a born educator. She's undeterred by the slightly edgy nature of their tactics. 'I've done it in front of police, they don't care,' she says. 'We only write educational info, it'd be madness to arrest us for that!' I nod in agreement – though I can't help but think about the frequent arrests of protestors for even daring to hold a placard in public, under the draconian Public Order Act.

The far greater crime, of course, is the one humanity is enacting on the natural world – and about which the Rebel Botanists are trying to raise the alarm. A recent major study by the Botanical Society of Britain and Ireland found that half of all native plants in the British Isles have declined in the last twenty years.[3] Yet many of us are unable to name even common wildflowers. We're caught in the grip of 'plant blindness', a myopia regarding the plant kingdom that renders us unable to distinguish between the rich diversity of species, and content ourselves that anything green is good – even if it's just a herbicide-drenched lawn or monoculture crop. The simple genius of the Rebel Botanists has been to open the public's eyes to the wealth of plant species that still surround us, even in urban concrete jungles.

I grab a piece of chalk and start scanning the ground for plants to identify. There's a dozen or so Rebels out today, inscribing the kerbsides near Plymouth's Central Park in the glorious May sunshine. Bluebells wash down a bank that's also covered with cataracts of sticky bud and tufts of cow parsley. I read the names of the plants already identified: *Vinca difformis*, intermediate periwinkle, with its starry mauve flowers; *Plantago lanceolata*, ribwort plantain, with deeply furrowed leaves; *Geranium robertianum*, herb robert, with its gangling red stems and pungent smell.

The Rebel Botanists are mainly amateurs, in the true sense of that word: the Latin root of 'amateur' is *amare*, meaning to love. You don't have to be a professionally trained botanist to develop a love for wild plants. There's no one-upmanship among the Rebels about botanical knowledge: just a refreshing honesty about the bewildering diversity of living things, with wildflower guidebooks and plant ID apps always at the ready to help identify what we're looking at. Gay, a retired bookseller, sports a yellow T-shirt depicting a large bumblebee. 'I'm not a professional botanist at all,' she says, although her late brother had been. 'I should've paid more attention to his botany skills while he was alive!' she sighs. 'I don't know much about plants, but I can pick up litter,' says Rachel, another Rebel, as she walks past with a discarded plastic bottle in her hand.

When I visit, Plymouth has recently played host to a tree massacre. In spring 2023, the Tory-run council cut down 110 mature trees in the city centre in the dead of night, to public consternation.[4] But in the subsequent local elections, the voters of Plymouth took an axe to the council, felling all but one of the Conservative councillors and installing a Labour administration instead. The tree-felling scandal resonated even for those choosing to spoil their votes, with one Tory candidate complaining: 'They've been drawing trees on the ballot papers, which makes a change from phallic symbols.'⁵ One of the Rebels, Delphine – silver-haired and pushing a bicycle – is wearing a badge that reads PROUD TREEHUGGER. I ask her about the felled trees, having not been to the scene of the crime myself. 'Brace yourself, it's horrible,' she warns me. 'Savage. Nobody wants to see it.'

In contrast to the ecological vandalism wrought by the council, the Rebel Botanists are trying to reverse the erosion of nature across their city. Over the past two years, their activism has evolved beyond walk and chalk sessions to also embrace guerrilla gardening, reviving local allotments as community gardens bursting with wildlife, and taking care of neglected pocket parks. An 'adopt-a-verge' project that Liz tells me about seeks to get residents to preserve their grass verges from overzealous council mowers. The overall aim is to banish the modern obsession with ecological tidiness – a compulsion to clear up every last corner, excise every green shoot poking through a crack in a paving slab; to chop, spray, plough, hew, exterminate.

At last, I'm pleased to be able to help identify a tiny fern that's formed a green necklace along some crumbling masonry: wall-rue, or *Asplenium ruta-muraria*. 'Small plant, long name,' grins Liz. 'Overcompensating, as far as I'm concerned.' In opening our eyes to such small things, the Rebel Botanists are helping cure society's blindness towards the natural world.

Healing

DAL KULAR, SHEFFIELD

'Unhealings'

Cooped up in this little terraced house, in this industrial
land no-escape,
my cells become red brick and loneliness, caulked to keep
a world inside, stacked against the elements and human-
creatures outside.
Bricks breathe but their breath is too thick. Opening
windows means inhaling the exhales of drills and diesel,
all night parties,
screaming children, screaming parents, blaring televisions,
car stereos booooming, buzzzzings, vibrationssss,
washing machines on high spin, invisible skunk fumes that
tease nostrils but fail to intoxicate me to elsewhere.
Twenty-four hours of the city's rhythm on repeat.
The trees have been chopped down and the blue tits no
longer call.

Unhealing is searching for sticks by a river and hearing
the words:
'Get off my land', and 'I'm going to get my husband
to come down here and shoot you!'

Unhealing is escaping the city to a campsite
and being called a paki by the owner
and being asked: 'Tell me one single place
which the British Empire did not make better than before?'

Unhealing is a White Lives Matter banner brandished
on top of Mam Tor, Derbyshire.
These unhealings jolt my soma, stir things I cannot remember.
Makes me want to turn and run. But where?
I'm in nature and nature loves me. I they.
Nature is not a white only space to be owned/tamed/
fenced/gamed.

Get used to this little Brown post-menopausal,
silver-streaked woman. Because here I am again.
Searching for sticks at the river. Again.
Camping my empire-survivor arse under our stars,
on your campsite. Again.
Being held by the wind on Mam Tor.
Again. And again.
I refuse your refusals of me. Again. And again.

Of refusing nature.
I know that when I escape the city and reach the hills,
the world feels possible again.
My ancestors feel possible again. I feel possible again.

Love notes to nature

'I am never not thinking about nature ... because I don't
understand a way we can be honest about who we are without
understanding that we are nature'
— Camille T. Dungy

Dear Nature,

Being with/of/in nature. Such a bodily felt experience between you and I, we. We speak in the innumerable languages of vibrations, ripples and waves, wonder and birdsong and dreams, ancestors and ghosts, and gusts of wind. Long time ago we didn't even need words, we just understood each other and cared for each other because we are kin.[1]

How do I write about this beauty between us, in the English language of my appropriated tongue? Words reduce the other-knowledges, other-knowledges found beyond the arrangement of letters, beyond ancient and sacred words which have been rubbed raw of magic, nuance and possibility. Your languages know nothing of letters and their ability to put people in their place. Perhaps the Roman letters and words which'll drip from my pen onto paper are too naive to express the massiveness of how we feel about each other. You are ancient after all. Been here for ever. Before words existed.

Last year while walking, you made me prostrate at earth's altar. This time I wasn't bowing to my guru. My left boot slipped beneath me, for a moment I flew but the air couldn't hold me. In a fragment of a second my world turned, crashing me nose first and forehead into ground. My lips became red-wet, hot as if you and I had just rough-kissed. This was a hard prayer. You brought me down to earth. I stood up in a different world. Concussed. Brain injured. Fatigued.[*]

[*]In 2022 I experienced two head injuries. The first one occurred on 31 March, on the first death anniversary of my mother where a rusty iron arch fell on my nose on my allotment. The second head injury occurred on 30 July when I was walking very slowly through an out-of-service outdoor sculpture, which I felt 'pulled into'. My left boot skidded and my nose took the first impact (in the same place as the iron arch) followed by my forehead, jarring my neck back, injuring my left shoulder. Taken away in an ambulance, this is the injury I'm still recovering from with the support of the Long Term Neurological team, Sheffield.

I think you were teaching me something, Nature. If I am nature, too, then maybe you are telling me how concussed we all are. How we need to shake ourselves awake. How we need to stop and listen and tell the story otherwise.[2]

On Stanage Edge, Peak District

'Other-wired / I walk edges, partitions, crumbled gritstone spines, a steel halo rings my soul / made by wild gods and stolen wishes'
— Dal Kular, *(un)interrupted tongues*, 2022

Dear Nature,
I remember who I am up here on Stanage Edge, this crinkled three-and-a-half-mile gritstone escarpment in the Peak District National Park. Right now, the wind lifts my hat to elsewhere, spinning my hair around my face like a typhoon. I feel the wind and sun etch their languages into lines of poetry around my eyes, making me feel more me and less of the northern city where I was born.

Years of walking my footprints into their carboniferous slabbed pavement familiarised me with the wonder of Stanage's inhabitants: the fur-blur of mountain hares through sogging mist, the tremolo from a curlew's throat quivering over my skin, that buzzard with a ragged left wing riding airstreams, sashaying cotton grass waving at the sunset, and the musk of purple heathering across the moors — a quiet fragrance on my lips. I think these beings recognise my footsteps. Footsteps which come from nearby, with soles holding memories of far away.

We communicate otherwise, you and I. In wordless ways that float across air, caught in a beak and shaped into birdsong, along gusts and through gales, whispering through layers of gritstone, transmissions through stars.

Here and now: raising my arms to the sky, my jumper lifts upwards, too, my navel finding escape above my waistband. Filling with cold air — taking in the Hope Valley below — I imagine my navel being my fourth eye, a little dent that sucks in the landscapes of now, and back then, and tomorrow. A little dent where I was once connected to the internal landscape of my mother, before she pushed me out in the front room of Northumberland Road, Sheffield, 1968, and our cord was cut. Back in 1938 in Null, Punjab, we both lived inside my grandmother until my mum was pushed out and their cord was cut.

Cords and cuts and edges.

Back then I was a speck of stardust. I wonder if my grandmother felt me, inside my mother, inside her? I feel you inside me, Grandmother. Did you ever expect to be on Stanage with me, now?

For hundreds of years, as far back as my palm could be read, my people were of the land of five rivers. Full of generational knowledges, they farmed the lush plains of Punjab's alluvial soil, to the rhythm of moon and stars and seasons between seasons. Landed-lives imprinted into the palm lines of my parents, into me.

I need to keep my ancestors close, remember their original ways of being in kinship with all beings, natural and free. The spaciousness of sleeping on rooftops under the Milky Way. I need to feel the hot pulse of land inside me, reorder my cells with big sky and barefoot again. The only way I can do that here is come to The Edge, to breathe and unbelong from all the places I've never belonged.

On The Edge, what would my ancestors think of me here? That I'm a future ghost walking my freedom, in the shape of Dalbinder, in the aftermath of empire? Perhaps I am practising a freedom I might never have had in the Punjab? A quixotic glint of flickering freedom that never existed? Their ground was

shaken, this time a sacrificial altar ripped and torn in two by the British Empire. An arbitrary edge blood-made. Nature hurt.

Cords and cuts and partitions.

I wonder if this is it — ancestral healing and repair — if this is the pull to The Edge? My land-practice of walking becomes a practice of remembering and following in the footsteps of my kin. Remembering the original landscapes of my mother and grandmother. Women who walked between villages and gurdwaras. Women who walked across partition lines. Women who died across partition lines.

Living through the brutality of the 1947 Partition of India, we women were not meant to survive. On both sides of the newly split Punjab, estimates suggest at the very least 75,000 women raped, mutilated and murdered.[3] Countless others were abducted, ended their lives by jumping into wells[4] or were killed by their fathers, brothers or uncles to prevent rapes, religious conversions and to restore family honour. Women. Missing.

My mother was ten years old when this happened. She survived. And so I survived too.[*]

Walking up here on The Edge – this wild partition between the Steel City and the Peak District – is a remembering, a recalling of how I am free to be myself in nature. In the now. Where all the layers of identity are blown away. I feel everywhen[†] at once – linear

---

[*]This essay is dedicated to my grandmother, my mother and to women of all faiths who were raped, mutilated, murdered or ended their lives by suicide during the Partition of India in 1947 and those who survived the memories and scars. I remember you. Nature remembers you. We heal together across times.
[†]everywhen: meaning 'simultaneity of times, where past/present/future are one'.

time, chronological time – colonised time collapses. When I remember my true nature, I'm no longer a mechanised, controlled human being; I'm the living miracle of my ancestors' hard-fought freedoms, living their dreams of freedom here, because I am not able to over there. I'm bringing them with me with every step.

I'm a mangled geography of happenings across times.

On Gometra, Inner Hebrides

Dear Nature,

> '... as women we have come to distrust that power which rises from our deepest and nonrational knowledge'
>   – Audre Lorde, *Uses of the Erotic*, 1978

You see me, love me, get me, recognise me as kin. Sometimes our most sacred encounters feel like wet lips finding each other in the un-civil twilight hours. When sleep releases us from being skin-bound. When we are too doze-fucked to pretend to be anything other than raw and untameable and uninhibited – ourselves. Dispossessed of words. Made of ether and glow. I feel my mind melt, my thoughts evaporate. Becoming something so elemental, so unrecognisable to myself that this is what liberation must feel like, what the real me must feel like, magnificent and mysterious. I'm made of sparkling dust, iridescent and impossible.

We all are impossible and luminous beings.

Nature, I am learning to trust my power. Your power.
  I'm reminded that I'm part of this interdependent eco-system – a mass of cells, fungi, bacteria, all the plants I've eaten, the air and the pollen and the pollution and the dust mites I've

breathed, the sun I've been warmed by. That I originated from the sea, and my body contains seawater and salt tears. A speck of me once lived in the sky, in a community of specks. I'm elemental and infinite. I'm an incredible feat of earth's imagination. An impossibility come true.

So are you. So are we all.

Perhaps our (im)possibility and luminosity comes from our deepest and most irrational and erotic knowledges? The knowledges that English language hasn't yet managed to word. The knowledges that help us to heal. That's what being in nature does for me, it unleashes the erotic, the chaos, and allows me to be messy and free. I don't find this same kind of freedom in the therapy room or even through words in my journal. Words get in the way.

This is how I feel when I'm leaning my naked self against a slab of rock on Gometra, a tiny Inner Hebridean island. Being wave-splashed over and over and over again. The city, the colonisations, the micro-aggressions, the shoulds, the partitions – are washed away. Disappeared. For a while. This is a practice of erosion – eroding the layers and forcings of what a racist, misogynistic and capitalist society wants me to be. These are practices of erosion I've used over decades – disappearing and dissolving that which does not belong to me. I'm not sure if I knew what I was doing back then. Now I know. This is healing.

In Ecclesall Woods, Sheffield

'If you are doing the right thing for the earth, she's giving you great company'

– Vandana Shiva[5]

Dear Nature,

I'm the rambliest rambler ever. It's the most natural thing for me to spend time in the woods, soaking up the bluebells. Here, time unravels from illusions and delusions, ceases to exist. I become this slow thing, no longer charging to be somewhere, timing how fast I can walk or how far I can get. I take for ever, however long for ever is, to get somewhere because of the need to stop frequently – to pause/be/see/hear/feel/listen. Sometimes I hardly get anywhere, sitting for hours on end. Lying on my back staring at clouds floating by. I become 'useless to capitalism',[6] – to the capitalism of nature as a place for adventure sports, as a commodity to be purchased, as a place to *do* instead of *be*. I don't need a forest bathing ticket or expensive gear to sit and eat a cheese and pickle sandwich on a fallen tree trunk. I don't need an end point, a map or a phone.

Like a wild flaneur, I roam aimlessly and purposelessly in these local woods – making relations with silky forklet moss, old man's beard, long-tailed tits and jays, sinking my bare feet into the ground layer of decaying leaves, ivy, fungi and hoofprints – imagining the secret life of underground mycorrhizal networks, feeding tree families. To become lost and startled. To go home full of wonder and awe, cells made of fresh air and tree hugs. To be made almost Dalbinder by nature. This is healing.

Nature healing as abolitionist praxis

'We believe that the only way to create radically safe futures is by harnessing tools of radical imagination, collective experimentation and expansive hope'
— Evie Muir, *Peaks of Colour*, 2022.

Nature healing must be considered as a decolonial and abolitionist praxis[7] unravelling and repairing centuries of harm. As white settler colonisation terraformed indigenous people's landscapes around the world, they tried (and often succeeded) to terraform psyches, imaginations and eradicate indigenous knowledges. While I believe I've had experiences of immense personal healing and reckoning in nature, they feel incomplete. I believe there can be no 'wholeness' to healing in nature for us as individuals or for nature if we cannot reckon with healing nature and nature-healing within the aforementioned praxis of abolition – of healing a racist society, of deconstructing extraction, dismantling white supremacy, capitalism and commodification – of standing in solidarity with 370 million indigenous people, who are protecting 80 per cent of the world's biodiversity on 20 per cent of earth's land and water.[8]

Looking back, I realise my time spent in nature has regulated my fragmented nervous system, helping me to find a truer version of myself. A truer version who more and more struggles to exist in contemporary urban society. I find it impossible to unplug in the city. The city makes me lonely, fractious and anxious. For me, ideas of healing and nature do not equate to a quick fix. Nature reveals my complexities, problematises my existence upon this earth, unravels the assumptions I make of myself, that society makes of me and asks me to question, to re-feel myself into new relationship with the world, with myself and with others, and to extract myself from the relationships and structures which harm me. A questioning of what it is to be a human creature in this world, at a time of great turning and undoing.

I can 'forest bathe' to my heart's content, and, yes, I am sure the trees will feel me, but I need to practise this in the wider social context. My dad once told me that my grandfather had prayed for all our future generations to come. That includes me. He knew the world didn't stop with him. Perhaps we all need to pray? To make our work a healing prayer for nature, for us as nature. For all future nature. This is healing.

Nature helps me to step out of my city skin and become something otherwildly.* As a Brown woman, being/walking/feeling into these landscapes I am taking control of my body and my psyche on my terms, extracting myself from a society of extraction and exploitation, from the *unhealings*. I can drop the layers of societal constructs, labels and forget my neurodivergence. It's no longer me that is too intense, too ill, too nuts, too Brown, too woman, too clever, too mad – it's the over-culture; a society that is so out of kilter that to fit into it I have to deconstruct myself to such an extent that I become ill. I'm undiagnosing myself from all the labels psychiatry wants to give me and giving them back as a diagnosis for society itself. Thank you, but no thank you. I'm not your diagnosis. I am wild, untameable and free. This is healing.

Nature loves my Brown footsteps and nature loves Black footsteps because they recognise them as fugitive and free. As surviving and thriving. Nature recognises the energy of our ancestors in our soles, of people who come from people who loved nature and worked in symbiosis with nature. Land is not static or immaterial. Land is awake, watching us, deeply feeling of our presence. Feeling our joy, play and imaginations for how a world can be. Us and nature = a beautiful *landguage*. This is healing.

Otherwildly is a word which arrived in me during a free-write, for the making of my master's dissertation where I explored the roots of my creativity, identity and wildness through therapeutic zine-making methods. Though I love the word *wild*, I was troubled by the colonial overtones of the word *wild* and the commodification and overuse of wild for marketing purposes, thus reducing its potency. I wanted to find another way to express how I experienced myself as wild and the wildness around me. As a Brown woman, silenced woman (so they think), I've experienced a lifetime of othering. Therefore, otherwildly reclaims my otherness and my wildness, creating something altogether otherwise.

Dear Nature,

It's taken decades for me to work all of this out. Mostly, I loved you as you've loved me. I've felt you in every-way and not one-way. Our relationship has been a wild whole bodily experience that refuses the separations of us and nature. Refuses the separations of mind/body/spirit/soul. Refuses to believe that you don't feel me or communicate with me. Being able to unravel, examine and explore myself as a being of nature, and my place within nature has led me to these understandings.

Kissing earth's altar was a hard prayer. Thank you for showing me that we are all nature-beings of immense healing powers and potential. In our collective concussion we've forgotten who we are, becoming fragmented, separated and made less than the magnificence that we are. You allow us to re-practise and repair our freedoms and fugitivity, to be otherwise than the capitalistic world wants us to be. I don't want to go into nature for healing or rest, to then re-enter a world that wants to strip me of my true self.

This is the kind of nature healing I want for all of us. The kind of healing that makes us useless to white supremacy, useless to systems of power and oppression. I want the kind of healing in nature that makes us question everything, to listen to the wisdom found in thin places, to discover the joy of walking barefoot on gritstone paths, to watching the Perseid showers dazzle the deep night, to snuggle down under an old oak tree and sleep, to laugh and cry with friends as we free ourselves over and over and over again. Through our navel fourth eyes, we can dream of all the connecting cords of who we are, ever have been, are becoming. Knowing that if nature is our original home, and we are nature, then we are already home. We always have been.

THE ARCHITECTURE OF BELONGING

CLOOTIE TREE

Often we return to nature to experience something bigger than ourselves. And often, across human history, we have gone to the trees: whether we look up to the sky to experience the numinous, or whether we look to the earth, trees help us extrapolate from our human perspective, and point to something beyond us.

The Romans recognised the north European veneration of trees. Pliny the Elder describes a druid fertility rite that centred around a mistletoe-bearing oak. Tacitus wrote of Germanic cult practices taking place in groves. And sometimes entire woodlands were sites of worship, such as Caill Tomair, which once grew outside Dublin before it was cut down by the forces of Brian Boru in AD 1000. With their roots to the underworld, and their leaves in the heavens, trees have always been the portal to another realm, somewhere to take the body so the mind can wander.

In Irish lore, hawthorn and ash trees can be a gateway to the realm of the *Aos sí*, the fairies and tricksters of Irish fables. People left votive offerings at the trees in the hope of buying favour from these capricious spirits. Reciprocally, many of these ancient trees still stand, surrounded by the desert of ploughed monoculture, so strong are the power of folk stories and spiritual taboo that even industrial agriculture won't risk cutting them down.

The tradition of leaving offerings at the tree was a less bloody version of the druidic sacrifices of bulls beneath the oaks, and has morphed into the tradition of wish trees, or coin trees, where people sacrifice a coin from their pockets, and hammer it into the creases and cracks of bark. Coin trees can be found across the British Isles: there is an ancient fallen tree on the Tar Steps in Exmoor, so covered in coins that its bark looks like the scales of a snake; an oak in the gardens of Bolton Abbey, on Isle Maree in Gairloch, which Queen Victoria visited in 1877; and an old sycamore tree near Mountrath, Co. Laois. This tree was originally growing by the side of St Fintan's Well, but when the well was filled in (by a Protestant owner tired of scores of Catholic pilgrims tramping over his property) St Fintan himself visited the site, and caused the well to remerge across the road, within the heart of the tree. To this day, the water rises in a hollow at the centre of the tree's branches, ten foot above the ground.

Clootie is the Scottish word for a rag. Clootie trees are sacred because of their proximity to sacred springs, whose aquifer waters remain cold (and, in a spiritual mindset, pure) whatever the weather. The waters of these springs have long been considered to possess magical healing qualities, and so rituals have developed around these natural resources that pull people towards them, in hope of healing. For hundreds if not thousands of years, pilgrims have visited clootie wells in order to circle them three times, say a prayer and hang a piece of cloth that had previously been wrapped around the body of an ailing loved one. The belief was that the person would be healed of their condition when the rag had fully disintegrated. These have always been popular sites: in 1869, Robert Chambers, the author of *Chambers Book of Days*, describes Craigach Well on the first Sunday of May as 'like a fair', with English, Scots and Gaelic all spoken as the pilgrims made their offerings on the trees and drank from the well.

Of course, as with cairns, there is controversy. Many of the few clootie trees that remain in the British Isles have been the subject of complaint, usually by people whose eyes get sore at the sight of them. This is the same disgust at human presence in nature that is evoked by cairns, but there is an environmental concern, too. These days, it is much harder to find strips of cloth that are biodegradable, or haven't been dyed with noxious chemicals, and so these trees are very often festooned with rags that hang outside of the carbon cycle. People do not seem deterred that this stubborn refusal to rot undermines the whole tradition of clootie trees, that the patient will only recover when the cloth has disappeared. And so today's clootie trees are an honest mirror of the world we have created, where old customs do not make sense in modern consumer culture. All sorts of clothing, from shoes to bras and the ubiquitous face mask have been found hanging by the wells.

In the north-east of Scotland, Munlochy Well is a famous example of the clootie furore. The trees that line the path up to the well have been covered in rags for at least fourteen centuries but early in 2022 it was discovered the whole site had been cleared. The owners of the land, the Forestry Commission, denied involvement, and newspaper reports pinned the clearance on a 'mystery woman', though how they worked out the gender of this person no one knows; some speculate that the job was too big for just one person. The clearance of the site, the designation of these rags from prayer flags to litter, caused a heated response from locals. When the *Ross-shire Journal* ran an online poll on people's views of the clean-up, they found that 80 per cent were unhappy, with just 18 per cent saying it was necessary. Locals claimed that this mystery woman would be cursed, though no one was specific about what such a curse might consist of, or which deity might enact it. To this day, on Facebook pages people are debating whether to put up cameras to catch the cleaners.

But outside of the sensationalist press reports, locals have drawn deep on the source of this clootie magic, and responded with myth. The 'Friends of the Clootie Well' was created to coordinate a group of volunteers 'that have an interest in researching, and caring for, the Clootie Well at Munlochy'. They organise sensitive, seasonal clean-ups of the trees, but, crucially, they run storytelling events, both at the site and in local schools, to strengthen the lore of the clootie. In the prevalent stories of our time, those told by billboards and commercials, print and social media, these rags can only ever damage the environment. But by telling the older stories of the land, these locals are watering the roots of this tradition, so that the real meaning of the clootie trees can flourish. As these stories spring forth from the mouths of those that care, clootie trees, rags and all, once again become the fruiting bodies of an underground network of traditional beliefs that find magical, healing properties in our sacred connection with the natural world.

11

Homage

SAM LEE, LONDON

'Awake, awake sweet England, sweet England now awake
Unto the land obediently, and let us all partake.
For our future now, is calling, all in the skies so clear,
So resound, resound sweet England, for our history's
always near.
Let us sing,
Unto this living story,
Let us sing.'
        – Adapted from the traditional ballad written after
the great earthquake of London in 1580, collected by
Vaughan Williams in Herefordshire, 1909

In 1903, at a tea party in Essex, the great composer Ralph
Vaughan Williams had an encounter which changed the course
of his career. An elderly farm labourer, Charles Pottipher (whose
name incidentally derives from 'Pied de Fer' – iron foot, or
strong walker), sang an old folk song called 'Bushes and Briars'.
'It felt like something I had known all my life,' recalled Vaughan
Williams. Questioning Pottipher further about the story of his
songs, he remarked, 'If you can get the words, the almighty will
send you the tune.'

This idea of song coming to us through holy acquisition, or a kind of divine downloading, presents a curious notion. That the tune comes from somewhere or something above, and the words from a material realm underground, or within us, suggests a metaphysical, spiritual relationship rarely discussed in folk song discourse today. It suggests plough-hands and land workers were merely the receivers, the instruments through which songs were channelled. Might folk song be a lightning strike of heaven meeting the earthly realm, a double helix of narrative and melody that's inherited, or contagious, leaping between bodies like an animistic armature, connecting and infecting a community?

In the days when they were ubiquitous, our ancestors were enriched by such land mantras. Discharging them was a daily practice undertaken from behind the plough, or below the cow. It was done in places of solitude, sanctuary and celebration, but always with deep sensitivity to when a song was called for, alone or in company. Transmitted from lip to lobe, from mother to son, father to daughter, each song was at some point received, adapted, honed, redecorated and made one's own. Each ballad was held in custodianship for a lifetime hopefully to be passed onto the next generation. This journey of transmission instilled into each 'songbeing' the accumulated traces of every inhabitant it passed through, animating each subsequent song carrier onwards in turn. The songs maintained their continuity by holding each singer to their lineage, while also providing a set of shoulders for each generation to stand on when they were sung. It was a potent accumulation. But an exceptionally fragile one, too.

Writing in this way about songs, with concepts of supernatural power and devotionality, gets a lot of kickback from the academic folk establishment today. They argue that many folk songs were pulp fictions generated en masse by semi-literate hacks in print sweatshops. They will attest that romantic pseudo-bucolics were churned out cheaply because, on the degenerate city pavements and at country fairs, that's what sold. And they may be right. But the sacred and the profane have long been bedfellows when it comes to the art of song. The material we have inherited in the tradition might be thought of as profane or, worse, simplistic. But it has been moulded by a timeless set of conditions: the need for humans to tell stories and for us to recite what is vital and resonant to our lives.

This tradition once formed the entire repertoire of songs occupying our ancestors' lives. It was communally self-determined, deciding what survived and what didn't. We have always been a song species and the first Victorian collectors, right up until today's gatherers of traditional song, were searching for those vestiges of an oral tradition that have existed until now, for ever. Although often changeable in their narrative and melodic structures, folk songs have always been testaments to the most pertinent facets in our lives. And until very recently, that often meant our relationship with nature. Once upon a time our fields and narrow ways, our riverbanks and bridleways, footpaths and agricultural thoroughfares would have hummed with the sound of songs reverberating from our community's songsters. These balladeers would have filled taverns, fields, milking parlours and farmyards, hollering tales of lives passed and our timeless connection to the land. A romantic pastoral vision? Maybe. But it's clear that in the first fifty years of the twentieth century, something in that irrepressible continuum of narratives broke. The fields started to quieten, the singing died, the well dried.

The last millennium's history of land rights has proved quite clearly that those with power are, in their pursuit of wealth, able to find ever more insidious ways to sever, sinew by sinew, the attachment to the land that we common stewards have long upheld. The landed establishment's war of attrition was aimed directly at the commoner's sense of land sovereignty, and they knew that repression of folk culture was essential to weakening the solidarity and resilience among the people they so often wished to subdue. By the time Vaughan Williams began his song-seeking, Britain was in a state of self-subjugation through centuries of egregious state policies, land reforms and enclosure acts. Indeed, the impact of those experiences is seen in the demise of these songs' relevance; their disappearance a direct result of a nation and society beleaguered, threadbare and lock-jawed. The ancient rites of song which had been central to our relationship with the land grew infertile, taken to the brink of extinction. Eventually, people stopped caring about those old songs and with every hard winter another song carrier took their bounty of land acknowledgement back with them to the land, unbequeathed and undocumented.

But at what cost? Once we forgot how to sing with the land, we also forgot how to protect it. Those fragile, selfless, adoring homages to the old ways held a whole lore of respect and reverence for the land. Yet we sacrificed them to the altar of opportunity and prosperity, drinking the Kool-Aid of an emergent urban culture which gave anything to leave behind the apparent misery of our impoverished and 'primitive' rural past.

Not long after the great disappearance of singers, the same quietening occurred on the land itself. Following the Second World War, campaigns to maximise agricultural productivity and changes in land management triggered a terrible decline in species. Some of our greatest singers — nightingales, skylarks, turtledoves, swifts and curlew — began a trajectory into ever-increasing scarcity. Once thick in the skies, now thin in the ears; as we stopped singing, so did our land.

What is a land without its song? Living in the times we do, we bear witness to a tangible crisis for nature where the decline in diversity and abundance goes unheeded by those with power, accelerating us towards a precipice of no return. Faced with such a crisis, how does song, especially *old* song, hold relevance and influence in a world howling for change and reconciliation? And if all that long-held ceremony through song has gone, how do we begin a journey of reawakening in our devotion for nature? What does a contemporary and relevant form of appreciation look like? Can we kickstart those old ecstatic feelings, reclaim an unashamed adoration? Could time outdoors result in the same endorphinous release, akin to those feelings of joy when we leave a great concert, or that sense of feeling touched, spoken to, and heard? And if it could, can it reach beyond the disparate ways and places enjoyed mostly by a minority of initiated and privileged people? Reading this means you are more than likely to be one of these people. But how does the wellspring of such unashamed nature bliss bubble up and flood the mainstream? Can this shift in appreciation leave the grassy fringes and hit the masses, becoming zeitgeist and de rigueur, commonplace in happening but invitational to a diverse and general public? If our biosphere has a chance it needs to.

In *The Dreaming of Place*, Hugh Lupton wrote:

> The land we inhabit is wounded, it has become desecrated as never before … and it will not recover until it has become, in some way, sacred again. Part of the process of re-sacralisation must involve telling of the myths of land-scape, re-storying and re-dreaming the land, using word and song to make numinous once again the mysterious ground that is the grandfather of all grandfathers, the grandmother of all grandmothers.

Could it be that the reclamation of our old song might sit some-where in the foundations of this reawakening? In our search for what a multicultural indigenous British identity could be, might we begin by paying some attention to the treasures on

our own doorstep? We have now had seventy-something years of a folk song revival. Yet the movement has mostly remained subterranean; hibernating from real popular attention, with the so-called establishment folk community over the last twenty-five years seeming especially unsure of the genre's purpose. But with climate and ecological breakdown the biggest threat to our future, you just need to look through the inventory of subjects in folk song and you have a ready-made list of endangered or threatened species. This ancient ledger reads not in complaint but as a reverential acknowledgement of each species' part in the order of things. With this roll call in mind, I ask where are our turtledoves, where are our larks and nightingales, where are our wildflower meadows, our crystal springs, our rivers clear, our forests deep?

These songs were our homages to nature in the true sense of the word. Homage derives from the feudal system of pledging reverence and submission to your lord; it's a contract of allegiance. Despite still living in feudal systems of ownership which prevent most people from accessing our natural heritage, these are surely the beings we need to be revering and in submission to, not in dominion of. We have fallen into an amnesiac disconnect from these very beings we depend on, allowing them to become strangers. Their vitality determines ours.

Homage needs new clothes and definitely a new soundtrack. When imagining what the simple act of 'humming' and 'homage' have in common I'm led to wonder what a British equivalent of the Hindu 'om' or 'umm' might be. A sound form that focuses our intentions on where the healing is needed; a native omage. Is there a singular mantra to chant or multiple ones, and could our old folk songs be its source?

My own quest has been to transcribe this nature power, or 'Old Wow' as I call it, into a musical language; to activate a practice that affirms and eulogises nature's sacredness – and its sexiness; to recover and restore the songs that can elicit desire to tend to nature's vitality as effectively as the music that seeks to elicit spiritual enlightenment and pleasure-seeking. Nature needs new anthems, and it needs us to sing them loud.

I call this work of re-storying and acoustic rewilding 'Songdreaming'. In concept, it's the working with old songs as the nuclei from which new stories can be grown, stories of our relationship with the land today and perhaps the future, too. Songs that celebrate the moments in nature that nourish us now. It is a neologism that rose from an old Devon folk song called 'Meeting Is a Pleasant Place', drawing on the state of mind I found when divining 'songlines' here in Britain. Songdreaming is a gesture of offering our voice, using old and new, improvised or chosen music while passage-making or self-made ceremony to induce oneself into soporific, unself-conscious, swooning adoration with nature. It's a love elixir. A sound potion-making. An act of whim and playfulness, theatre and alchemy. It replaces the ridiculous with the delirious. It has no rules or conditions and can be participatory or a passive thought-form. Wherever and however it occurs it's a conjurer of storied paths and sonic-psycho-geographic maps. Songdreaming reveals highways of half-remembered, half-imagined thoroughfares bubbling with ancestral dialogues. It turns us into a vessel but also the tuning fork; it's what we, as a storied species, have always meant to do.

I've had many moments when, in retrospect, I can see that the veil was crossed and that I was in a state of Songdreaming. But possibly my most profound experience happened one Easter Sunday back in 2016. I was leading a music and nature connection residency for about thirty people in the renowned centre for alternative learning called Embercombe in Devon, and we were on our final day together. We'd gone offsite to some mixed pine and deciduous woods to undertake a silent, barefooted, blindfolded practice that has extraordinary powers of opening up sensory and kinaesthetic connection. I'd saved my favourite offering until last. As the exercise came to an end, finding ourselves in a place where words could not adequately convey what had just happened to us, we took off our blindfolds and gathered together, arms over shoulders, to reconvene and quite instinctively we began singing. We fell into one of the anthems we'd learned over the long weekend, not an old song but a small round about breath. The first prompt that something special was happening came from a chiffchaff that flew straight up to the branch directly above us and began emphatically singing, putting a grin on everyone's face. But what happened next can only be remembered as a moment of complete affirmation that our song and ritual making were effectively sacred and necessary.

It was March and the weather had been kind to us for much of the week. At that moment, the sun shone low through the trees, piercing a gap between two tree trunks. Without warning, a biblical downpour descended on us in our little clearing – and only us, not seemingly over the woods beyond but just in that small spot of ours. I had my back directly to the sun and, as if by magic, a miniature rainbow appeared within our circle, crossing from one side of the group to the other, bridging the circle's sides. It was radiant and yet barely bigger than our group. As the optical laws of rainbows dictate, only myself and the two people on either side of me could see what was happening, and we gasped in shock. So we started to rotate around in caterpillar step. As each person came into position, with their back to the sun, the rainbow appeared to them and their jaws dropped in awe and disbelief. As we completed our rotation the sky found the tap. And as suddenly as it had come, the downpour stopped, and the rainbow vanished. We had kept the song going throughout this brief elemental encounter as all of us knew instinctively, like Charles Pottipher had said, that we were receiving encouragement from the land and the heavens. Old Wow approved.

For meeting is a pleasant place
Between my love and I
I'll go down to yonder valley
It is there I will sit and sing
I'll sit and sing for you, my love
From morning noon till night
And from morning noon till night my love
It is there I will sit and sing
Time draws circles round our lives
Put your arms round me
Measure England's miles with me old friend
Our song is our release
What will your four scores foresee
From the mountains down to the sea
Songdreaming opens wonder paths
Enchant us with your melody.

Our folk narratives have long been informed by the trauma of our separation from the land, inflicted by those with power who, to this day, demarcate and control our alchemic bond to nature. They are filled with lament, separation, injustice – and yet always hope. Songdreaming is a resurrection of this impetus. It invites an invocation of those who have walked before us and invites us to step where they may not have been able. It's an evocation of what lived and lives beneath us but always within us as inheritors of our forefathers' and mothers' land loves and system rages. The simple act of taking songs back to the land, walking with them, rewilding them and letting their intergenerational outcries run free, acts to broker a new sense of permission for all. Songs resurrected and played with in this way are our guidebooks, our hymns and treasure maps to buried caches of enchantment in nature. But they are also bolt cutters, barbed wire breachers and passports to our long-fenced-off great garden. Songs used in this way act as an orientation when we feel lost as much as when we feel the loss. They are compasses, conductors and companions, talismans to console us in moments of ecological grief. But most of all they are lanterns illuminating us along paths we know we need to walk lest they are for ever closed in front of us. This simple act of singing while walking, of carrying song as companion, renders the ground transparent to our past and sweeps away the oppressive constraints of any transgression. Trespassing becomes pilgrimage, peregrination; it becomes permissive and all-powerful.

I write no prescription for the ingredients of this practice and no blueprint or guidance for how it should or shouldn't happen. And, most importantly, in no way do I claim to have invented this Songdreaming idea. I only borrow its conceit from cultures and vocabularies where it still occurs; the indigenous and tribal cultures around the world whose lore of the land, despite many attempts by society to break it, has within my lifetime survived. There are also many elements that are drawn from gypsy and traveller song carriers, the very last of whom I was lucky enough to be a student of in my time as a song collector. Those singers, of which only a handful are still left alive in the British Isles, were our last connectors to an ancient oral tradition and link us to an ancestral form of divination and conjuring of the land. It is to them that I pay homage in this work but also from them that I learned to cast my own spells as a singer, as a land listener, as an activist and a provocateur for change.

Of course this practice already occurs in so many idiosyncratic ways all the time. It is carried on under a multitude of names in all sorts of places by individuals and groups, both casually and formally, religiously and agnostically alike. We see it shine in Glastonbury's Festival, Appleby's Horse Fair, Stonehenge solstices, Padstow's Mayday and the West End's *Jerusalem* among many other instances. In each rendering, it intoxicates us into a state of connection to place. Britain is blessed with all the creativity and heritage needed for such work – there we do not lack. But to conjure all the right ghosts, pluck all the right heartstrings, shiver every neck hair and wrestle the algorithms all at once … well, that's quite the cocktail of magicry.

As much as we need nature, nature needs us. Nature needs us to show up in our most songful, artful ways. The real progress begins when enough of these summonings amalgamate and trigger a tidal surge. Their gathered iridescence glowing so bright, so irresistible, that at some point their inherent demand for a better way collectively prevails over the laws and lawmakers that legitimise and prioritise nature's decimation. This is when the dreamwork really happens. It's then we wake giants, the dragons stir, and the revolution of priorities, of what needs saving, can begin.

So let us pay homage first to those singers who have passed on to us this canon of verse; a practice of gratitude and belief. They are our great benefactors to this cause. And if you ever find yourself in Ingrave, Essex, put your ear close to the ground. You might be lucky enough to hear some incantations emanating from around the grave of Charles Pottipher. And if you do hear something uttered from below, it will be as though you've known it all your life. But remember, too, to offer a song of your own back.

Your voice,
Your voice,
Is necessary.
We're weak alone,
But strong as many,
So sing with heart,
And fire in belly

WILD SERVICE IN ACTION

BECCA AND THE RIGHTS OF THE RIVER AVON

Becca doesn't come across as a natural rebel. 'I've always been a bit scared of authority – of being told off. But the river is a place where I don't recognise any authority.'

For the past two years Becca has campaigned on behalf of the River Avon and its swimmers, a journey which started with a breaststroke and led to a battle with a multi-million-pound water company and a recalcitrant mayor. The Conham Bathing Water Group has forged an alliance of swimmers and scientists, ecologists and campaigners to fight for the recovery of an enchanted and beleaguered stretch of river which is loved by those who use it and abused by those who exploit it.

When we meet in the spring of 2023, Becca is fresh from a showdown with the mayor of Bristol; her application for a stretch of river at Conham to receive Designated Bathing Water status was stymied by a byelaw which the council claimed to prohibit swimming in the river. 'It actually referred to Bristol harbour, which is three miles away and very different from the verdant idyll at Conham.' Even in the industrial harbour, the swimmers were having none of it: 'I joined in with a few pro-test swims which I have to say were quite fun – with the har-bour master chasing us in his boat and us all running away in our swimming costumes. But it's a totally different experience to Conham, where we're applying for bathing status.'

The importance of such designations is currently more pol-itical than it is recreational: from one outflow alone on this stretch of the Avon, Wessex Water have dumped the equivalent of twenty-four days of sewage over a nine-month period, and the river suffers badly from agricultural phosphate pollutants. Designation would shine an interrogation lamp on such activ-ities, obliging the water companies to conduct regular testing of the bathing area – and report the inevitably embarrassing results.

It also highlights other absurdities about England's relation-ship to rivers and the laws surrounding them. 'The harbour bathing company tests the water, as do we, but without bathing water status this does little to nothing to actually address the pollution. Meanwhile the byelaw prohibits swimming, while simultaneously inhibiting action to address any of the reasons the water isn't considered safe for swimming. It's a logic loop to insanity.'

Becca is not a traditional activist. Rather, her campaigning emerged from her immersion; prompted by a reconnection with her childhood river, the Monnow, during the Covid lockdown of 2020. 'That first lockdown was strangely idyllic. I hiked every day, swam, slept out by the riverside. It was scary at the same time, but I felt so *vital*.' By the time the winter lockdown hit, Becca had moved to Bristol and taken to swimming every day for her mental health. 'I couldn't believe the difference cold water made to me – what a gift.'

It was there that she learned from other swimmers about the extent of sewage pollution afflicting the nation's rivers. 'I felt wounded because I'd taken a swimmable river for granted, and guilty because I realised I'd not been upholding my end of the reciprocity. Rivers had given me so much my whole life and through ignorance I hadn't done enough in return.' That ignorance, she believes, resides partly in England's poor access rights. 'Even now I don't know the Avon enough – you can't follow it even between our swim spot and the city centre. It's the same for so many rivers. What's missing is access.'

Becca first experienced a right to roam in Sweden when some friends took her mushroom picking. 'That changed the direction of my life. Being able to wander freely was not only incredibly liberating, it showed me what we've lost here and highlighted my lack of knowledge. Learning how to forage, especially mushrooms, is a slow process, but the baseline of public expertise in Scandinavia is amazing because everyone has an opportunity to do it.'

Back in England, she decided to follow a similar trajectory with her river: learning as much as she could about it regardless of her lack of access, and diving deep into unfamiliar fields of water ecology and environmental policy. 'The imposter syndrome was bad, but there came a bit of a *fuck-it* moment when I thought, if not me, who? And if not now, when? Passion is my qualification.' More rigorous accreditations have since followed, with a master's in public policy and a dissertation focusing on the concept of legal rights for rivers – partly inspired by Paul Powlesland's work on the Roding (discussed in Chapter 5) and campaigns for recognition of the rights of the rivers Frome and Don. She's fascinated by the practicalities of making such rights manifest. 'At a recent river festival, we invited people to speak on behalf of invertebrates, or flora, we gave them blindfolds and asked for those perspectives. Humans were included too, of course, but as co-actors in the ecosphere.'

But Becca's enthusiasm and diligence are in marked contrast to those who wield the most power over the river's fate. Having drummed up the 5,000 signatures required to trigger a debate at a full meeting of Bristol City Council, she was excited they might finally see some positive action from the relevant authorities, and prepared accordingly. 'We were so prepped ... we went through so many drafts, thought of every single counter-argument – parking, safety, you name it, and had answers for everything. A councillor from each party then responded and they were all supportive – it was incredibly emotional. But it remained the mayor's decision and it was as if he hadn't really listened at all. He deferred, then kicked the issue into the long grass, saying that the harbour byelaws would be reviewed in a few years. But a little later he announced a harbour swimming partnership with a commercial outfit who now charge seven quid a time!' Meanwhile, at Conham, a sign appeared declaring that swimming in the river is dangerous. 'The last word was promptly scratched out and is periodically replaced with things like "wonderful" and "great for your mental health" ... which then get rubbed out by the council until someone adds a new one.'

Once upon a time Becca might have listened to such admonitions and taken their authority for granted. No longer. 'Rivers have empowered me and unlocked a mischievousness that didn't exist in other parts of my life. And swimming in skins through that awful winter of 2021 built up a baseline of confidence that somehow enabled me to chase away other anxieties and to stick my neck out, unqualified as I felt. I'm in a feedback loop where rivers give me the confidence to fight for rivers.'

12

Belonging

BRYONY ELLA, KENT

My heart quickened as I arrived at the edge of the rainforest. A warm, humid heat was lifting through dense layers of ferns and palms, bright greens surrounded by trees I could not name, spiked red epiphytes clinging to their branches. Shards of light touched woody vines coiling to the ground, meeting roots robed with gigantic fallen leaves, golden and brown. Above me the late morning sun was rising into blue sky scattered with drifting clouds. Around me, the air was filled with noises new to my ears, alien and exhilarating. Branches crashed, wings hummed, lizards scattered leaf litter. I revolved on the spot, eyes open wide.

This was the homeland of my father. It had been decades since he had set foot on the island, but the memories had stayed to old age, imprinted from childhood. He had often talked of his wish to show me this landscape and ever since I had learned the words 'Trinidad and Tobago' I had dreamed of this day. But now, finally standing on ancestral ground as an adult, the scene before me was discombobulating, saturated with sounds and shapes I did not know. I felt dizzy, and alone.

I remembered to breathe.

Behind me the distant toots of cars signalled the city. As a child I had been taught that forests were safe spaces full of magic;

cities less so. I was raised in England by my white mother who adored the natural world; every walk with her invariably ended with pockets full of acorns or shells, feathers or lichen. She encouraged my sister and me to marvel at the different colours, shapes and textures of nature, delighting in folklore and fairy tales of woodland creatures. I adored these fantastical stories, revelling in the sense of wonder they brought to every corner of my world; they opened my imagination to the magic of invisible networks and interactions of more-than-human beings. When I was about eight we left Yorkshire to move to a village in Kent edged by forest and orchards. There, we were encouraged to play outdoors. Joining a motley crew of about six local kids, we would spend hours playing 'Catch me! Catch me!', which was essentially Hide and Seek except that we each became a different animal and would call to the seekers from our hiding places as wild dog, or owl, or cuckoo; whichever animal we felt like that day. Occasionally, we filled the forest with monkeys and tigers. We were little wildlings, howling from trees and yipping as we ran through bracken, covered in mud with leaves in our hair, filled with the unbridled delight of being young and outside.

I missed that exuberance. Now in my late thirties, over the past six months I had walked every day through the same Kent forest while our family navigated the surreal world of palliative care. Suki, our mother, had been diagnosed with terminal cancer. Logging off from the noise of urban life, I yearned for the trees that had once known me as a child. There, I could be safe to grapple with the disbelief that surged through my body. In the city, the sterility of the hospitals suffocated me − there was no space to scream. But in the forest I became a small, wild thing again, the trees, with their familiar summer coats, my companions as I stumbled through the processing of each stage of the illness. As leaves turned to a golden falling, I observed the solemnity of their release, their branches bare and clear against the sky. One by one their leaves tumbled to the cold, frosted ground until, one morning, basked in the bright winter sun, my mother died.

Two months later, on impulse, I decided to travel to Trinidad. I hoped it would bring some kind of perspective on the nonsensicalness of it all; everything reminded me of her absence and I did not know how to return to the life I knew before. Around the time of the funeral my elderly father, Michael, had been moved into a care home as his dementia progressed; when I visited, he would forget that I was sitting with him, each time surprised by my appearance when he looked up. My heart was broken. The disintegration of such fundamental anchors of belonging destabilised me; who was I without them? Where was 'home' now?

As a mixed-race child growing up in rural England, as the only non-white member of my family — my father living in another part of the UK — my sense of belonging had been fragile. At primary school I had become painfully aware of looking different from most of the other children, and my mother had tried to protect me as I struggled with experiences of feeling othered. Around the time of her illness, the UK's political and social landscape was rupturing. Brexit had thrown into stark relief societal divisions regarding who belonged here and who didn't and, almost overnight, the subtle racism that I had learned to navigate transformed into violent outbursts from strangers. I was told to go back to where I came from more times than I care to count. A man shouted 'n——' in my face as I left a supermarket. While painting a mural inspired by the English oak, a passer-by furiously accused me of 'turning a wall African'. Over just a few short years my sense of belonging had been shaken and I began to wonder whether I might find kinship elsewhere.

I arrived in Trinidad and Tobago with a distinct sense of disembodiment. I wasn't *in* my body, I was lugging it behind me, a heavy, clay-like, numb thing caked in emotions that I could not articulate. I had thought the trip might offer some respite but when I landed in the capital I had found a different kind of overwhelm; the rush of people, thrum of cars and pounding of sound systems had pressed down on my senses so that it felt impossible to hear myself think. As an only child, his parents long since passed, my father had only distant relatives on the island. I met them, and they were friendly and curious about the world I had come from. Yet despite their warm welcome I felt a sense that this wasn't my culture, nor was it my community; I felt a little bit like a fraud. The fact that I did not have, nor, due to complex administrative issues, could have citizenship played on my mind. What did it mean to be Trinidadian? Could I rightfully claim this heritage? After a week or so struggling with this strange loneliness, I decided to explore the countryside. There I hoped the forest might offer a different kind of sensory overload to the city, one that would not demand my attention but, perhaps, awaken it.

Standing at the entrance to the rainforest, I noticed a gigantic silk cotton tree towering in the distance. I decided to clamber my way towards her, ducking under orb spider webs, narrowly missing biting, barbed 'jigger' vines and skirting a babbling stream concealed by undergrowth. It was an overgrown, winding trail and I had to stop to re-find it several times. Eventually I reached a small clearing. Looking up, I swung unsteady on the spot and staggered. I had never seen such a tree as this in my life. Her crown must have been at least 150 feet high with branches circling the forest, wide and open like an umbrella. Armies of spiked cones travelled across her trunk, studding the spines of enormous roots that ribboned around me, while along her lower branches streamers of feathered vines and flowers clung just out of reach. A short, spontaneous laugh of delight burst from me; the first in a long time. She was magnificent! What had she witnessed from such a height, at such an age? This tree must have been hundreds of years old, surely unperturbed by the comings and goings of human beings and our short, chaotic lives. A thought crossed my mind, and lingered. Had my ancestors known this tree? Momentarily disorientated by the strange sensation of past meeting present, I sat down and leaned against one of the roots, careful to find a smooth section of bark.

What now?

Shifting on the ground, I stretched out and took big lungfuls of air, sweet, warm and woody. I opened my rucksack and gazed at the art materials I had packed, unsure of where to start. What on earth am I doing here? Recalling an exercise once shared with me and not knowing what else to do, I decided to give it a try. I picked out a pencil and sketch pad and closed my eyes, tentatively making small marks every time I heard a noise. Moving around the page, I orientated the sounds in relation to where I was sitting, faltering at first as I struggled to quieten the judgemental chatter of my mind. Soon I picked out high-pitched chirps behind me, which became light curls at the bottom of the page. A falling branch to my right turned into a heavy scribble along the edge. Songs began to twirl around the top of the sheet, following notes as they lifted before stopping abruptly and then beginning again. I became aware of their distant replies – faint strokes –and in close proximity cicadas ticked with dashes and dots. As the sounds resonated throughout the forest, my focus began to expand further outwards. This felt good. Gradually more creatures resumed their conversations; frogs commenced their croaking – hooped marks hopping in one corner where they met soft coos – undulating lead swirls. As my ears became attuned to the chorus of songs and scuttlings, a soundscape of intertwining shapes began to layer across the page. After what must have been half an hour of blind drawing, I opened my eyes to take in a page of scribbles. Quite beautiful, really, if only for the recording of a brief moment in time.

I decided to see what else I could notice. Revolving on the spot, I took in the root before me, its stripes of brown and green rising like a wave before folding into the earth some ten feet away. Adjusting my pencil, I honed in on a small section and began to shade the bands of green that flowed down the bark, following the tiny bumps and fine golden lines that ran between its grooves. As my pencil brushed over the tooth of the paper and streams of graphite rippled across the page, I felt happy to give such a minute area of the forest so much undivided attention.

By now the sun was high in the sky; I was losing track of time.

Shuffling around to lean against the root, I adjusted my eyes to focus outwards and picked out a heavier, softer pencil, making sweeping marks every time I noticed something move. A woodcreeper scurried up a trunk searching for insects — small vertical jumps. Hummingbirds hovered, glittering green — a light shading mid-air — then darted — a flourish of graphite. Ginormous black bees zipped low between blooms — tight, concentrated zigzags. Flashes of birds I did not know — emeralds, scarlets, cobalt blues, chestnuts — flitted between branches. My pencil twirled across the page, trying to keep up with the explosion of animation. A small green bird alighted on a branch near me, crowned with an extraordinary red tuft. A gang of chattering parrots took flight, circling into the sky — thick, swooping strokes. Lizards scurried — fast flicks across the forest floor. Leafcutter ants with parasols of vegetation marched in line — tiny dark dots, footnotes on the page. The sunlight illuminated butterflies dancing through the undergrowth — delicate horizontal waves — my spirits lifting with them.

I decided to stretch my legs and followed one of the silk cotton roots down a slope to a small clearing where leaves shot upwards in vivid green and dropped lines of waxy, scarlet flowers edged with yellow lips. Transfixed, I watched as a tiny ruby-red hummingbird hovered over one of the flowers and dipped its beak into the nectar-filled cup. With my pencil I began to follow the curve of this flower to its pointed tip before sweeping down to draw the row of blooms hanging underneath and, after some time, I became aware that my breath was syncing to the rhythmic flow of the pencil. I pondered on this invisible exchange between myself and the plant in that moment; as I inhaled I drew in oxygen released by this plant; as I exhaled, its huge leathery leaves pulled in my carbon dioxide. Intentionally now, I synchronised movement and breath, flowing the pencil down the page as I took in a deep breath, outlining a small section of foliage on the way, and then arcing upwards to add more detail as I exhaled. The experience became almost meditative as my pencil looped around the page, a fine row of bloom patterns holding court in the centre.

Eventually I returned to the shade of the silk cotton. There, I found my eyes drawn to the shadow shapes that fell across my sketchbook and, tracing them, felt a childlike glee in following the quick flickering pattern fragments of the canopy as it rustled in the breeze. It was impossible to capture the shapes, but I enjoyed the playful dance of trying, a memory stirring in the back of my mind of a children's story about catching shadows.

And so the afternoon stretched on, with each mark seeming to weave me further into the tapestry of the landscape. I experimented with how to draw scent, texture and temperature. I crouched under shrubs and lay on my stomach to find different perspectives. I pulled out a pocket mirror to peek inside the folds of a bromeliad, searching for tree frogs.

The artist Paul Klee once said, 'a line is a dot that went for a walk' and that was exactly what it felt like I was doing. Just a few hours ago my whole being had felt condensed to a tiny dark point, a shocked-to-stillness clay body retreating from the human world. Now it felt like the act of drawing was playfully guiding me out into the vastness of the more-than-human world, calling my attention to the myriad life forms that tumbled and glided and scurried around me. Or, rather, alongside me. These simple activities decentralised my ego, opening me to the realisation that life carried on, ever-moving, always growing, relentlessly *living* — regardless of the pain that I clung to. I was not the centre of this universe but a part of it. The sensation felt almost like space was expanding around me, the present moment evolving into a new experience of presence into which it was safe to not only unfurl my grief but also absorb the sheer beauty, wonder and (dare I say it?) joy of being alive.

This wasn't some kind of sublime out-of-body spiritual experience — it was visceral. Beetles tickled my knees, nesting birds shat on my rucksack, mosquitos guzzled my blood. Spiked prongs scratched my shins, the sun prickled my skin and beads of sweat rolled down my face. This new felt awareness was as messy as it was glorious. That afternoon I became a part of the landscape, admiring how the sun glistened my brown skin golden, how my arms and legs became roots and branches traversed by insects, how my face rippled with palm and sky reflected in the stream. Wonder stirred there, an old friend I had not known for many years, and pleasure surfaced through camouflage, my stillness a portal to the sensory dynamism of the forest. The simple act of putting pencil to paper had drawn me into a state of flow that, rather than distracting me from my grief, somehow seemed to articulate it. As a human being I was alone in the forest, but I was not lonely. The body that had carried me was gone, but her love of the natural world lived, still.

When I returned to the UK the world was on the cusp of pandemic lockdowns and, a few short weeks later, my father was moved out of the care home with suspected pneumonia. On April Fool's Day, just as I was jumping in the car to get to the hospital, I received a phone call to tell me that he had died.

Three years to the day I returned to Trinidad with my father's ashes, finding the tallest hill in San Fernando, where he was born. I found a ridge that overlooked the sprawling city and in the far distance, Venezuela, the homeland of my great-grandmother. As I opened the box a light breeze lifted his ashes into the heat of the day, intermingling with music carried from a birthday party over the hill. I remember feeling a distinctly peaceful acceptance that afternoon as I watched black king corbeau vultures glide silently overhead, guardians of the border between the living and the dead. Together there then, we witnessed my father returning into the world.

During the intervening years I had joined the UK in mourning life as we knew it, the passing of family and friends, the pain of separation from loved ones when they needed us most. There was some solace in the collective experience of loss then; we were all moving through the surreal suspension of everyday life. As my drawing experiments progressed, I began to share them in small groups. I named it 'wild drawing'. Although nervous at first — the practice was so simple — participants reflected back my own experience of re-enchantment with the intricacies of the natural world, feeling replenished by the close observation of nature. Artist residences and collaborations with climate scientists, eco-therapists, movement practitioners and ecologists followed, and in cities and countryside we gathered together to explore the fluidity and interdependence between human and nature.

Guiding wild drawing walks through the city challenged my own notion of nature as being something 'out there'. With magnifying glasses we studied the minute worlds within worlds of lichen curving around grooves of tree bark, woodlice clambering over mossy tops, spider webs tugged by gusts of wind, drops of ink spooling into rain spots on our page. These experiences deepened my sense of always being *in* nature. Wind, rain, sun and earth, moths, beetles, crows and dandelions; nature pushed through the cracks of concrete and filled our skies. Coupled with the embodied quality of this practice — touching, listening, tasting, smelling and observing the natural world — wild drawing was renewing my relationship not only with nature, but also with myself.

At around the same time I discovered that the word human comes from the Latin word *humus*, meaning earth or ground. This inspired new conversations in my collaborations with scientists, intersecting not only my creative practice but also my private spiritual explorations. Although I do not belong to a faith group, the passing of my parents had certainly awakened a curiosity in the concept of afterlife. In the West, so much of what we learn about nature comes from narratives that treat it as something 'other', to be extracted, tamed and owned. I began to wonder what might happen if we instead engaged with an embodied clarity of ourselves as humus; as organic beings temporarily animated as human yet destined to be reclaimed by fire, water or soil, reintegrating into the same living world that our human systems are currently degrading. If we cultivated an understanding of our very beingness as land, surely this would reveal the impossibility of our *not* belonging and in so doing perhaps transform our relationship to the nature crisis and the systems that perpetuate it? This has now become a central question in my art practice. In *Figuring*, Maria Popova writes on how 'we spend our lives trying to discern where we end and the rest of the world begins', constrained by borders and boxes brittle in their rigidity and unreliable in their promise of security.* And yet, the earth to which we ultimately belong

*Does it feel more secure to place the weight of our belonging to a nation or to earth? In 2022 a report by the Institution of Statelessness and Inclusion at

constantly forms and reforms, the bodies of our ancestors transformed yet forever moving with tides and tectonic plates, hurricanes and rivers, glaciers and volcanoes. Every particle is in constant motion.

Wild drawing has become my own small act of Wild Service; a gentle, embodied observation of the dynamic world that has unexpectedly gifted me with such a profound sense of belonging that the human illusions of hierarchy by which I used to define myself have lost their potency. I am sure that it is a practice I will continue to evolve throughout my lifetime; there are infinite ways to unfurl deeper, more expansive understandings of what it means to belong in nature. Perhaps you might be inspired to try

Middlesex University and the Global Citizenship Observatory revealed that over the past decade the UK has stripped more people of their citizenship than any other country apart from Bahrain.

the activities I have shared here or to embark on your own creative explorations of the natural world. Either way, I encourage you to play. Connect with your inner child's ability to delight in the (re)discovery and wonder of nature of all shapes and scales. Experiment with different ways of moving through the landscape, notice the new perspectives this brings. Draw yourself back into the living world by heightening your awareness of and attentiveness to your bodily contact with nature, and allow any grief for its loss to surface alongside the pleasure of its majesty. These exercises do not need to be complex, nor do the artworks need to be shared. In fact, I would encourage you to remove those pressures of performance and perfectionism. Prioritise instead the intimacy of the practice; Wild Service is an invitation to awaken the ancient, wild and sensory part of ourselves that intuitively knows we belong to the fate of the natural world. And that one day each of us will indeed return to where we came from.

WILD SERVICE IN ACTION

IBRAHIM AND THE SEABIRDS OF COQUET ISLAND

Coquet Island is a small island about a kilometre off the north-east coast of England. Closed to the public, the small ocean rock is a haven for 40,000 pairs of seabirds including puffins, terns and gulls. Seabirds spend most of their lives at sea, resting together on the water in 'rafts' between flying and fishing, far out to sea, unseen and unrecorded. They return in the spring to breed on the island where they make their nests in burrows and on the ground, and the island is a sanctuary away from hungry hedgehogs, badgers, foxes and rats. It is the only place in the UK where roseate terns breed.

'Getting on the boat, you are waiting and dreaming about the island, and then your dream comes into reality. I couldn't believe what I am doing. I felt like I needed my eyes to be bigger to absorb everything.' Ibrahim is a reserve warden for the RSPB, and a Syrian migrant who came to the UK on a scholarship in 2011 to study for a PhD. He soon discovered that the project wasn't what he was looking for, stuck behind a computer while he wanted to be closer to birds and closer to nature. 'I didn't come from Syria to sit in an office, I came to see the culture and to see the birds and to feel the birds.' But it was when a fellow student, who was studying seabirds on Coquet Island, left their work that Ibrahim got his chance. Having helped with their work, he knew the project well, so when their supervisor asked Ibrahim if he would be interested in continuing the project, he said, 'yes, I can start tomorrow'. Soon after he was on his way to Coquet to spend his first night on the island.

'That first night was a test, will you love it, can you survive in such an environment? I didn't want to be inside, I was walking from the jetty to the lighthouse, just going around and around and watching every aspect about the island. There were no birds because it was after the breeding season, it was just grass growing after a long summer.' He was asked to come again for a week in 2015 and by 2016 he had begun his first year on the project, living alone on the island, monitoring birds and gathering data for the RSPB. 'Two thousand and fifteen was the year that changed my life, I lived among the seabirds for the next four years.' It was during this year spent in close observation that Ibrahim began to learn the language of these wild birds, picking up the nuanced differences between their calls. 'As you start to understand this, you feel more connected to them … the new creatures were coming into my life, I started to understand how they were talking and what they were saying. I watched them bring gifts to each other, each of the hundreds of nests doing a different thing.'

He describes a nest that they monitored with a small camera, an intimate insight into a family's life: 'We put a nest camera inside the roseate tern box, watching the nest on the monitor, minute by minute. Then I started hearing a call from the female sitting in the box. She was calling a special call, I could tell it was something different from the other calls. Then the male turned up to the nest.' He watched the monitor as the male tern moved from the back of the female to the front, then back again, and again and again, caressing her. 'He kept talking to her, like he was saying push, push. And she laid her eggs, and then they started dancing together.' As he watched these birds, he saw their personalities emerge from behind their scientific classification, and thought of all the nests on the island, with the different personalities forming individual homes: 'You are watching this and you learn that you are connecting to nature … when the eggs hatch, they are calling like they are happy. It's not just surviving. There is something else there.'

Ibrahim watched the same box for seven years. He saw how the male progressed from an awkward, fumbling father, struggling to feed fish to the chicks, to become an expert dad.

But after several years tragedy struck. Since 2021, bird flu has had a large impact on breeding seabird colonies in the

UK with tens of thousands of birds dying from the Scottish Highlands to the Scilly Isles. Originating from poultry farms, the virus has spread to wild bird populations, badly impacting breeding colonies where birds are nesting in close proximity to each other. The family that Ibrahim had felt a part of, that he had watched for seven years, succumbed to bird flu, and the screen on which he watched the family flourish went empty ... 'Unfortunately, the first roseate tern died from bird flu in that box. We were grieving like part of the family.' One of the chicks died first and then he watched as the dad also succumbed in front of the camera. The pain in his voice as he tells this story is still raw: statistics transformed into visceral loss through his personal connection to this one family of birds.

'That left the mother, but she stayed in the box, and rarely left it. If she was going outside, it was to wait for someone to come back. But he never came. The mother died, eventually, but not from the bird flu. She stopped eating or going out of the box.' She didn't show signs of flu; what Ibrahim felt watching her behaviour and how he empathised was as if he was watching someone die from sadness. 'She was above the dead body of her partner, as though she was saying, "stand up, you can fly again". We see it happen in humans, we die from sadness, but I saw that it can happen in animals, too.'

At the outbreak of the bird flu, the staff could not go to the island because of the risk of spreading or catching the virus. For Ibrahim this was a difficult experience, and he likens it to missing our family when they are sick in hospital. He wanted to be with his family.

Over time, a scientific study evolved into a relationship founded on understanding and an empathetic link between Ibrahim and the birds, forming a bond of belonging. Yet these bonds are neither acknowledged nor understood by the system that controls Ibrahim's status as a migrant. Thirteen years since he arrived legally in the British Isles, thirteen years of legal employment, thirteen years of forging a natural bond with his environment, he is still waiting for his UK residency.

When asked about his feeling of belonging, far from his birthplace in a land that refuses to acknowledge his legitimacy, he says: 'I wish I was a bird so it would be easier.' He describes a pair of Mediterranean gulls which come to nest on the island, similar to our common black-headed gulls, which every year say, 'we are nesting here and we are laying eggs. And every year the black-headed gulls fight them, recognising that they are different, making their life harder. But when something scares the flock, they all fly up together and all of them are flying as one.'

Ibrahim is now in the process of his residency application, but it is taking ages. 'It's been thirteen years and I still can't get it. I came here legally, without anything from the government, and I have always worked. It is difficult for me to understand sometimes why this is happening. But nature is helping me. That is what has given me a feeling of connecting to nature – it is more than passports and skin colour. I have learned a lot from this. It has made me really strong; I see us all, animals and humans, as one.'

13

Inheritance

ROMILLY SWANN, SOUTH OXFORDSHIRE

I appear to have inherited a problem. I have agreed to rent some unkempt land next to the community orchard where I graze my sheep. The fences are far from stock-proof, it is also criss-crossed with paths and awkwardly divided by an area of well-established woodland. On each side of this dividing wood is rough pasture and scrub and I am wondering how best to manage such a rural triptych: the needs of sheep, visitors and nature.

I cast an eye over the mosaic of grass and meadow flowers and, as an experiment, I imagine a line heading away from me into the distance. Such a line, if imposed, would have the power to direct and contain humans on the one side, and grazing animals on the other. I imagine the luxuriant, carefully laid hedge that could be this line's future and wonder if it is right to assert a boundary here, on what used to be common land? A while back I asked Eric Hartley, a very kind and knowledgeable local historian, if he knew anything about the common, and he lent me a book by J. H. Baker, written in 1937, called *Land of the Gap*. According to Baker, the area was once 'an extensive tract of barren land', the only remnants of which are the 'enclosed heath' and 'Cherry Common'. I observe a twisted cherrywood stump, decaying, but still pointing defiantly skywards, and ponder how much has changed since its heyday. This land, though considered barren, would have provided for the commoners. But where are they now? The fact that I am standing alone, not another soul in sight, feels significant.

As with all commons, there was a time when folk wandered unhindered here, gathering resources and grazing their animals. Because their lives depended on them, they cared for these spaces. If anyone dared take too much from the common store, they risked upsetting the balance and breaking the lore of the commons. Responsibilities for land, crops, natural resources and animals were woven into this cultural governance. I look at the pattern of desire lines still here today, worn into the sward. These are not footpaths in the legal sense, but clear tracks honed by hundreds of feet following memories imprinted in the land by the footsteps of others. If I plant a hedge I will change these patterns and obligate visitors to alter their habits and memories. However removed we humans are from our rural heritage, we still create these navigational constructs by which to travel and return. We speak them to others, we share maps and our experience of a place. This is how we belong.

Compromising that sense of belonging is furthest from my intention but, like other farmers, I have to think about the many and varied visitors in the countryside and the inevitable clashes of interest. It's thought-provoking when someone anonymously leaves their very expensive Porsche in a field entrance. Even though I am well equipped to shift such an encumbrance with the tractor's loading forks, I don't. Out of kindness and fear of an expensive insurance claim, I am forced to wait for hours in the field until the owner returns.

Car infuriations aside, sheep farmers inevitably have particular welfare concerns. At Cherry Common I keep a primitive breed of sheep in order to increase biodiversity on marginal land and to help educate and rehabilitate people. But also as part of a valiant attempt to reinvigorate our moribund British textile industry, I keep them for their fleece. Though there are some who think there should be no sheep in the countryside and that we should grow our meat and fibre in Petri dishes, the truth is that this once barren land could not sustain vegetable growing or commercial agriculture and there's not much scope for bison or effective scale rewilding here in the densely populated Thames Valley. So here I am with the challenge of grazing sheep in fields with high footfall and all its associated problems. Dogs leaving excrement or releasing their inner wolf. Litter binding a wether's gut. Fences and gates left open, or broken. At all times, day and night, I dread the call to report sheep on a road, or covered in blood, or trailing a leg, or dead. I also dread the anger from visitors if I ask them to control their dog, respect a gate or an area with vulnerable species. It saddens me, but I try not to despair as I understand that capitalism and the industrial revolution generated this baseline culture of resentment towards farmers and landowners. It is obvious, too, that this is due to disconnection with nature and the rural landscape of which all communities would have once been inextricably a part. I wonder if they're actually embarrassed, or ashamed of their ignorance and disconnection, and I try not to make things worse. In fact, I want to make things better. I think back to my hedge and wonder how it might help or hinder these stresses.

By drawing a line in thorn and directing people through a gate, I am clearly dictating where visitors and animals can and cannot go but, curiously, I am also offering freedom. On the one side, freedom for walkers to leave their dogs off-lead and, on the other, freedom for sheep to safely graze. Crucially, though, in the liminal zones that an established hedge creates, there is also freedom for nature to thrive. Visitors will still be welcome on either side of the hedge, but this new line would mark a change in land management that would need respecting. On one side they will be on what was an old way, marked on a 1761 map, which leads to the road and eastern meadow beyond the little wood. On the other they would be among my very convivial sheep.

Even the word hedge is fraught with these tensions. From the old English 'hecg' meaning a fence, we also get phrases such as 'hedge fund', 'hedge investment', 'hedging your bets' or 'hedging to avoid giving a direct answer'. I wonder why medieval folk adopted the word 'hedge' to mean dodge or evade; and then, in the modern period, to invest in opposing markets to insure against one's losses? Aside from being able to dodge or hide behind a hedge I guess that, as here, a hedge can mark a divide that requires investment on both sides.

Alongside a history as a common, these cleaved and vexing acres have much to teach me. For a start I could do with learning all the wild species present in this space and how they interact with each other, the soil and weather, with grazing animals and humans. I want to understand the fields in my care as well as I can. And I wonder for a moment if inheriting land, rather than renting or having common rights, might in some cases lead to complacency. I think of an estate nearby where the landowner is absent: how can he know or care about the thousands of acres he has inherited if he's never there to experience it? Without inherited assurance or knowledge passed down through generations, or years of experience of this particular field and how visitors use it, I too feel ill-equipped but duty bound to honour the complexity of this space, all the native inhabitants and those who pass through it.

Cherry Common, like every field and boundary in England, has a story. It has a folk history, an unwritten lineage of intricate relationships with local people and travellers. I don't know the languages that were spoken, the songs that were sung or the traditions, customs and values observed in this place through this time, but beneath my feet lies a story left by distant forebears who dwelt here. They may no longer have a voice but there are various ways we can catch glimpses of their lives. For example, we can fly planes equipped with LiDAR (light detection and ranging) equipment over a site and see minute altitude changes. These lumps, bumps, dips and furrows reveal that this particular land has never been ploughed. Because of this, archaeology shows up clearly. We can see where roads, homes and field boundaries once were, but the people who built these things can never tell us what they knew of this place, how best to manage the land to maintain the delicate balance of harvesting enough food and resources for the human residents without harming the natural ecosystems on which they depended. We will never know the cultural value systems they created to thrive here before economic pressure and engines made farming a deceptively easy way to abuse the fragile compromise.

In past days of oral tradition, stories were told down the generations as cautionary tales to keep succeeding generations safe and well. Stories about giants, witches and dragons, or where herbs and mushrooms, poisons or medicines could be gathered with ill intent or good. A powerful legacy of local identity, lore and wisdom evolved, long before land had owners or could change hands with wills and money. These days oral inheritance is all but lost and mostly unattainable from web pages or books. Local lore or indigenous wisdom can only be gained over time and experience, careful observation and respect. I ask myself what I wish had been passed on by the now silent voices that once resounded here. The world and its climate is swiftly changing; would their wisdom even help me now?

In the spirit of Wild Service, however, my deliberations about this hedge are not solely centred around humans past or present, or even sheep. I wish to provide a refuge, a byway and sanctuary for wildlife and homeless flowers. Defended by mother thorn, the shyest of the wild can creep and blossom. A hedge

stands protective, a celebration of diversity, complexity and interdependence.

A butterfly, a meadow brown, lands on a greater knapweed flower and I watch for a while and think: here is an insect and flower that I know well but that for most children today would be unfamiliar and unnameable. Without an inherited or contextual story the unnamed cannot live in our minds. They remain outcast from the constantly evolving, virtual ecosystem in our heads into which we plug our experiences of nature. Friends, be they plant or creature, need a name by which we know them.

My father was an avid botanist and though he didn't think much of children, endeavoured to teach me the Latin name of every plant I came across. This included the wild service tree, *Sorbus torminalis*, when over forty years ago I stood with my father as he explained to a hedge cutter that a tree with pretty leaves shaped like spiky hands, a wild service tree, should not be cut down. Latin names are the same and universally used the world over and not being afraid to learn them turned out to be my most useful inheritance. This and a good working knowledge of plants and nature through study and drawing leaves me unable to properly comprehend the blank disconnect I often observe in the children I work with that are mostly new to natural habitats. Robert Macfarlane and Jackie Morris's book *The Lost Words* beautifully illustrates this tragic loss, but it still cannot replace the love and connection built from time spent quietly observing nature. I mean *really* quietly, in that way that you have been still for so long that nature has forgotten that you are there. Only then will the magic begin to flow and fill you with awe. You might see the meadow brown unfurl her coiled tongue to drink from the knapweed flower. Then, if you take the time to look even more closely, you may see an ant below, suckling on the knapweed's extra floral nectaries, which you might not have known were there. This time, this space, which in our frenetic world could easily be mistaken for idleness, I consider to be vital moments of profound reverence and grace. In the days before enclosure, when the commons filled our larders, these moments might have cemented our sense of belonging. This is what every child should know. Because without such a sense of kinship with nature, the land they inhabit will suffer.

I feel that we need some help from cultures which are still connected to indigenous thinking. I reach for Tyson Yunkaporta's book *Sand Talk*. This book was my companion while I lived in a caravan on Cherry Common for six weeks of lambing this year. It is a provocation to cultures that have been divorced from indigenous thinking. Sand talk refers to the Aboriginal custom of depicting a world view drawn through lines in the sand. In the hope that I might find some help with my dilemmas, I have been chewing over the concepts he describes and, inspired by Tyson's invitation, 'to alter them to match your own local environment and culture', I have been slowly adapting the ideas to fit this land, and perhaps the wider problems I see in our relationship to land and nature in British culture.

Tyson teaches five different indigenous thinking styles by linking them to the digits on a hand. Right now this is useful, as it makes it easier for me to remember and carry them with me wherever I go. My task is to link them to the land before me. Following Tyson's example, I let my thumb rest against my baby finger which he asks us to understand as kinship mind. I read how this little finger represents a child, who learns to relate to those around it and the natural world. As Tyson describes: 'This puts children at the centre of the family and society, the ones that make relationships happen, tying everything together into a social system.'

Kinship mind seems to me to be about this relation: the idea that we're not isolated individuals, but, rather, exist in constant interplay with one another in a web of collective responsibility.

Though dependent on where and how we grew up, how we were treated and how we learned to treat others, it universally links our lived experiences to each other and the land. Our relationship to nature evolves through this time. Every child takes their lead from the adults around them. If adults don't feel comfortable and confident in nature, neither will their children. As baseline understanding and knowledge of nature has shifted with enclosure, urbanisation, inadequate education and human-centred preoccupations, children have inevitably become increasingly alienated from their natural surroundings.

Kinship mind rightly puts the child at the centre, but as a reflection of society it is our shared responsibility if children reflect our failings. Though we all have a right to make mistakes, we have a collective responsibility to underwrite them when we do. It reminds me that it is OK to not know how to be in the land, as long we are open to learning. Following Tyson's lead perhaps the first Wild Service rule of thumb should be:

We are all responsible for each other.

I touch my thumb to my ring finger: Tyson explains that this represents story mind. He asks us to contemplate the first stories learned from our primary caregivers, how the world opens up to us from these stories, and how a stable society is dependent on understanding how these stories interweave. This finger reminds us how all other connections radiate out from this initiation. I think of what I learned as a child, of botanical, herbal and ecological tales and knowledge which allowed me to begin attending to details in the land, unveiling its 'hidden' stories. Every plant and creature is interrelated and by being there can tell an intricate story if you choose to read it.

The ability to read these stories forms the bedrock of our understanding of place, and allows us to act in accordance with its logic. Looking around me, I read the changes in flora, the stories of the ecology: the ring of brambles around a twisted cherry stump where blackberry-plump birds had perched in a once grand tree, excreting seeds; a patch of nettles, where animals have enjoyed the shade; a tell-tale curved band of droughted plants that marks the route of a long unused trackway. I think through less obvious complexities, interactions, hidden benefits and philosophical fruits that might arise from my hedge and how I might communicate these to others. And I land on the second rule of thumb:

Learn to read the stories of the land.

I put my thumb against my middle finger that Tyson explains represents dreaming mind. Tyson describes this as the creative reaction to the land around us, using 'metaphor, images, song, dance, words, objects'. Our land culture in England is depleted, the harvest songs and May dances largely forgotten, but the core of these cultural activities is the gathering of the community around a central focus: the work of the land. Culture becomes the connective tissue between our lives and the wider context of place. When we sing, work and laugh together we learn the power of reciprocity and collaboration; we become more than the sum of our numbers.

I imagine people coming together to help plant the hedge, balancing the interests of nature, livestock and community. Conversations will be had and heartaches shared. Someone might ask if anyone heard a cuckoo, nightingale or lapwing last year or share fears of a late frost biting cherry, plum or apple blossom. We need this. It helps us through grieving and hardship, sorrow and joy. It eases loneliness and lends us the energy, despite setbacks, to notice, check in and care for all the beings around us. Culture emerging from nature, community coming from culture, and from community: service. With this flow in mind, I think of a third rule for Wild Service:

Come together to create a culture of care.

Now I touch my thumb to my forefinger, representing ancestor mind. Here I think of inheritance. Not the inheritance of money or land but a different wealth altogether: inherited wisdom, traditions, customs, skills and crafts. Craft is emblematic of the thread that was broken when we turned our back on the land, the inherited values we forgot amid a swiftly changing world.

It is the loss of this inheritance that makes me worry about our collective failure to intelligently serve this land and all that share it. Craft is crucial to our visceral connection with land, so as I cogitate I make a flower crown. I was taught this skill many years ago by a farmer as a thank-you for my small part in rescuing a cow from a bog. And many times since, I have passed it on to others.

I walk around the field carefully selecting suitable flower stems and with practised hands I twine them together into a braid. Each flower is thoughtfully chosen, triggering my story mind, fondly recalling names, uses, associations and connections with each plant as my fingers work. Finally, I weave the last stems into the first flower heads, forming a circle and completing the crown. This skill, like so many rural crafts, has been handed down from unknown hand to unknown hand, generation by generation, and was passed on to me by a stranger. I feel grateful to have been shown this craft and I put the crown on my head to wear in honour of every human link in that chain of knowledge that brought it to me. The crown represents the lineage of knowledge and interaction with the land, with each twist in its circle reliant on the one that came before and the one that comes next to hold it together. Rule number four honours this inheritance, and reminds us to play our part in passing it on into the future:

Hand on what you cherish.

Lastly, represented by the thumb, Tyson introduces the idea of pattern mind, which he describes as 'the skill of seeing the whole and not just the parts, a big picture understanding of how things work'. The dominion we have chosen to wield over nature has not only disrupted many of its patterns but distanced us from our ability to recognise them. Yet the continued existence and wellbeing of our species, and the natural world around us, depends upon this ability, not to impose, but to discern and interpret these patterns. If we take the time and patience to observe nature, its patterns become clear, the Fibonacci spirals of the pine cone and circling hawk, the symmetry in the moth's wings, the ancestral pathways of badgers, the habits of crows, and if we step back, we observe how these patterns have evolved out of a wider pattern of necessity that holds them all in balance. Pattern thinking utilises all four rules of thumb to discern the patterns of balance that exist in one particular place, and urges us to act in accordance with these dynamics.

Just as Tyson sees pattern mind as a way of 'seeing entire systems and the trends and patterns in them, using these to make accurate predictions and find solutions to complex problems' so I realise that this land can serve as a microcosm for wider possibilities: its patterns, problems and solutions helping guide, in its small, quiet way, a new relationship to land across England. And that even our smallest acts of Wild Service are empowered when made part of a wider, cultural whole. Standing among these wildflowers and buzz of insects, I acknowledge the power of nature and my wish to work with rather than against it and decide on a final rule:

Act within the patterns of nature.

This type of thinking is helping me with the whys and wherefores of planting an impenetrable line of shrubs. It also makes me want to check the 1761 map again. I am not surprised to see clearly marked hedges, both sides of the old way. With no sign in the field, I peer into the woods alongside and there, against the fence line, are two parallel banks marking the position of two original hedgerows. So, from reading into the stories of this land, I discover that I would actually be putting a hedge back. I wonder when and why it was removed and what instinct and intuition had spoken to me through the millennia, along with reading the land now? What had made me imagine what had once been? Is this what happens when we tune into place?

I stand in my flower crown at the end of the dreaming hedge, where it meets the dividing woodland between the two meadows and I ponder. I am aware that this story of a field, a hedge and inheritance is about to become a lot more complicated. This land is part of Hardwick Estate, which is owned by Sir Julian Rose. As a tenant farmer I live and keep my sheep here. But this established, very English hierarchy is currently in the process of being dismantled and replaced by something radical.

A group of estate tenants, including myself and Sir Julian's daughter, recently attended a conference on the Isle of Skye. We travelled there to hear the latest news of land reform, right to roam, community land ownership and governance in Scotland in order to help us understand the complexities and pitfalls of handing over an estate into community ownership and governance here in England. Very soon, the owners of this estate will disinherit themselves, and hand the land over to a community-run charitable trust. As I look back along my imaginary hedgeline, I think of the responsibilities that are soon to be ours. I see that it is all too easy to become oppositional and place landowners on one side of a divide with everyone else on the other. But what if the accepted norm is turned around, and the landowner asks you to step up and govern the land you live and work on? By taking that responsibility, are you also taking a side? Boundaries are important pragmatic agricultural necessities, but do they need to be divisive? As a farmer I worry about the scorn that I might incur from the wider agricultural community if I support right to roam. Like other farmers, I currently feel ill represented, misunderstood and distrusted. This angers me: I know and care deeply about the land I farm and I know that farmers across England also stand in their fields, assess, read and think about the land and, despite horrendous economic pressures and capricious political directives, do their best.

By sharing some of my thoughts about a hedge, land management, sheep, human visitors and the wild inhabitants that have no voice in this debate, I hope to ease some of the polarity. Because through the prism of Wild Service, with Tyson's Aboriginal knowledge in hand, ultimately we all want the same thing: for land and nature to be healthy, productive and connected to the community. While tending my flock and the land in my care, I speak to hundreds of visitors to help convey and understand the complexities of history, politics, economic pressure and practicalities of opening up access. I draw upon my experience with sheep, lambs and land to better understand the realities and sensitivities around animal welfare, protecting wildlife and the impact of increasing numbers of visitors. Like other farmers I am painfully aware of the risks of opening up access to nature. There will always be people who bring insensitivity and ignorance into vulnerable landscapes, with disastrous results. As a mother and teacher, however, I feel that these risks are outweighed by benefits in the long term. Children have inherited a baseline understanding that land and nature, other than on footpaths, is only accessible to landowners and therefore

have frighteningly little knowledge, interest or investment in how to preserve it for future generations. This has to change and we must take risks to bring it about.

I look away from the hedge, beyond the dividing woodland to the eastern meadow, which is triangular and has a footpath through the middle. Nature is swiftly reclaiming this part of the common and in its wilding beauty I have stood and pondered many times, wondering what might be the best way to manage this awkward piece of land. If I fence it to contain sheep, it would exclude people from enjoying a picnic, which has long been a tradition here, or prevent them closely observing the nature of their environment. If I don't have sheep grazing it, I would have to mow every so often to maintain it as it is. Like the hedge, this meadow fills my head with queries. Queries that swiftly flow into the issues posed by the right to roam and Wild Service. But with Tyson's thought patterns in mind, it dawns on me that the wild inhabitants of this meadow along with the dividing woodland would not be too detrimentally affected, and might even benefit if the use of the land were shifted towards giving human visitors freedom and responsibility. Perhaps this humble meadow and tangled grove, like the estate they are part of, could defy the accepted norms of inheritance and set a precedent to catalyse long-lost ways of thinking? Like more enlightened places elsewhere, this could be a bit of country-side where people feel welcome and free to spend time enjoying nature's magic, in the knowledge that they are also part of it and empowered to act as custodians of it. By feeling welcome and wanted, they could watch the seasons turn and, by sharing what they learn, create a better, healthier life, for communities and nature together.

My reverie is disturbed by voices: a father and daughter are approaching along the path. They stop and I share some of my thoughts with them. After a while the child asks enquiringly about my crown. I kneel down beside her, taking the crown from my head. I tell her the names of the flowers and why I chose them. Mallow, clover, daisy, buttercup, knapweed, honeysuckle. The father listens and smiles as I gently place the crown upon the child's head. This is my gift, her inheritance.

THE ARCHITECTURE OF BELONGING

BOTHY

Squirrelled away in every bothy is a logbook, a record of its visitors, a collection of handwritten experiences, thoughts or poems to be shared with its future residents. These books speak of the lineage of temporary residents, they fill the bothy with the spirit of those gone by, but they also link us to the origin of bothy culture. Because in 1965, when a man called Bernard Heath was staying in a deserted shepherd's cottage in Backhill of Bush, forty miles west of Dumfries, he found a hidden logbook and read a suggestion that someone set up a club to preserve these crofters' shacks from ruin. Good idea, thought Bernard, and that summer he brought a group of friends to another deserted farmhouse in Tunskeen, near Galloway, where they repaired it, for free, for everyone.

At the end of that year, Bernard and a group of like-minded people met and agreed to form a club to preserve many of the deserted crofters' cottages, and the Mountain Bothy Association was formed. The minutes of that meeting were published in the association's first journal and included a crystallisation of their purpose: 'To maintain simple unlocked shelters in remote mountain country for the use of hillwalkers, climbers and other genuine outdoor enthusiasts who love the wild and lonely places.' Today, around 3,700 volunteers work weekends and holidays to repair roofs and floorboards, to install rudimentary insulation and stoves in around a hundred bothies across Scotland and Wales. And thousands more use them every year.

In today's commercialised industry of nature connection, an arms race of log-burner jacuzzis, wi-fi-connected shepherd's huts and luxury treehouse Airbnb retreats, the culture of bothies is refreshingly spartan. Because they are miles from any road, no taxi will drop you off at a bothy; you have to get there under your own steam. No bedding is provided, no mattresses or towels await your arrival. Most have a fireplace or stove and are near a natural source of water. You'll be lucky to get a toilet, or outhouse: the most bothies usually offer is a spade, and guidance of how to bury your business in an ecologically sound manner. If the biscuits are stale, you won't get your money back, because you never paid to stay.

The bothy code is equally sparse. You use a bothy at your own risk; no one is liable for your actions other than you. You are asked to leave the building clean and tidy, and as a nice touch that goes to the heart of bothy culture, you are asked to leave kindling for the next visitors. You pay your warmth forward. There is a strong culture of sharing in bothies, a traditional ethic that there is no such thing as a full bothy. No matter how limited the space, no matter how late newcomers arrive, space is always found. This is pragmatism before it is idealism – the weather conditions can be so harsh in these remote areas that shelter can be a matter of life or death. So everyone inside the bothy knows they have a duty to nudge over. The coldness of the conditions is directly proportionate to the warmth of your welcome. Bothies practise empathy.

The Mountain Bothy Association have listed the code of bothying on their website, but they did not create it. The ethics of bothy culture emerged organically from the people who used them, and had been around for at least two decades before the association was formed. In what is today called the Proletarian Revolution in Hillwalking, the 1940s and 1950s saw many working-class young people taking to the hills and openly flouting the trespass laws of Britain. Walking had primarily been considered a well-heeled pastime, and the moors and glens and mountains of Scotland, still owned to this day by little over 400 people, were the preserve of stag-stalking, grouse-shooting and fishing expeditions, not so much an industry as it is today, but more a practice of favours among a moneyed elite.

But these working-class men had returned from war with something of an expectation for a new future. And what the government wasn't going to give them, they resolved to take. They walked where they liked across mountain and dyke, and they often stayed the night in the remnants of the crofters' cottages left over from the time of their grandparents. And if the doors to these unused spaces were locked, they would jimmy them open so they could sleep the night. Over time, in spite of resistance from landowners and their gillies, the sheer scale of people using these deserted cottages made it pointless to try and stop them; together, a community of strangers had created a kind of de facto customary right, a lore that superseded the law.

Fast-forward seventy years and bothies have become integral features of the Scottish landscape, nodes in a much wider network of how the Scottish understand their relationship with the outdoors. What began with these lockpickers of the 1940s has now turned into a force of volunteers who have become so integral to the fabric of Scotland that they were awarded, in 2015, the Queen's Award for Voluntary Service. Bearing in mind that several bothies that had been occupied were on land that the queen herself owned, this is a striking anecdote of how opinion shifts in time and action; the landowner awards the squatter for overriding her exclusionary legal rights.

This is the journey that freedom takes. The empty crofters' cottages were the gravestones of a culture destroyed by the Scottish clearances, where a few aristocratic families evicted the locals and forced them into waged labour in the cities. They were repurposed by young people with a desire to be closer to the land they fought for, willing to break the law for what they knew, in their bones, was right. But it is the work of the Mountain Bothy Association that can teach us the most. Long before the Scottish Land Reform Act gave them a legal right to walk, swim and stay in their countryside, a small group of volunteers asserted their moral right, by actively caring for these cottages. They stepped over the legal fiction of exclusive ownership and claimed a stewardship over the places they loved but did not own. This service won them their right to access it and though it took decades for the law to catch up, they had already built a new structure of relationship to nature that was more complex, nuanced, pragmatic and idealistic than the blunt legal fictions of ownership. The open doors of the bothies unlocked the Scottish countryside; they opened people's minds to another way of being within nature. Each bothy stands today as a monument to the philosophy behind a right to roam, their roofs and walls serving not as the infrastructure of exclusion, but as the Architecture of Belonging.

Epilogue

Within the fragments of ancient woodland which still pock-mark our strange, beleaguered country, there resides a forgotten tree whose berries taste like sweets and whose leaves resemble hands.

The wild service tree, *Sorbus torminalis*, is 'the most local and least known' of our native arborea.¹ Yet for a time it held a central place in our culture. Its wood was treasured for its colour and strength. Its scarlet fruits flavoured our beer. And, once bletted by the first autumn frost, it gifted its berries as treats to be hawked at village fayres and sought out by sticky-fingered children who, as a result, became masters of where each tree would grow. Such knowledge was no doubt jealously guarded. An unwritten, backwoods lore shared cautiously with younger siblings and only the closest of friends.

The prized berries resemble those of the medlar tree, which the propagandists of 'improvement' were so keen to keep out of reach of the commoners they dispossessed. And they held a similar value. Indeed, John Clare, the great poet of that dispossession, wrote a dedication called 'The Surry Tree' which extolled the wild service's virtues for the wayfaring poor: 'tawny berry rich though wild ... Where hermits of a day may rove and dine / Luxuriantly amid thy crimson leaves'. In Clare's native Northamptonshire, the tree's branches were used as part of the annual beating the bounds ceremony, performed by villagers to demarcate the boundaries of the parish, and ensure land to which common right still existed had not been illicitly enclosed.

As such uses and rituals have fallen into neglect, so too has the tree which enabled them. Today, the wild service tree is scarce. But we don't know how scarce. Nobody has thought it important enough to count.

Clare's use of the word 'surry' for the tree is related to the Old English root of service, 'syfre', denoting religious devotion, a form of liturgy.[2] It is from this word that we derive the notion of a church service and from which this book takes its concept of Wild Service: a notion of ecological devotion which belongs to no religion, and dictates no singular creed. Wild Service recognises no borders and observes few boundaries. It does not distinguish by birth, or birthright. It is a dedication to be given, not a condition to be proved.

Throughout the pages of this book we have seen Wild Service manifest everywhere from the seed bombs sailing from Adrian's catapult, to Ibrahim's love for a dying family of terns. Wild Service was the only guest at Nadia's childhood conservation group and the partner of Paul's joy as the sand martins returned safely to their rescued nest. Wild Service is what had Amy running after her neighbours in a panic to hand praise for 'her' apples back to the tree which bore the fruit. It is the reward of the farmer Nicola coaxed to cease his ploughing, and the ensuing gift of a fresh clutch of lapwings barrel-rolling in the sky. Wild Service is the thread connecting people and belonging, community and care, guardianship and culture. Its wellspring is our reverence; its contract our homage; its gift our inheritance.

As Romilly discovered when cogitating on her gate, Wild Service poses a different set of questions to those which have long predominated on the land. Am I serving nature's interests when I plant this hedge, or my own? Who and what am

I excluding, or enabling, when I do? It expands the community of interest beyond the individual, or the rubrics under which they might currently be obliged to labour. And poses questions of the landless, too: is my dog's desire to charge through this heath more important than the nightjar which might be roosting there? Is my wish to warm myself by a fire more important than the moss it's situated on, which perhaps took generations to establish there?

Throughout the course of the Right to Roam campaign we have grown used to hearing (always in the patrician voice, and always when talking about the 'general public') that *rights come with responsibilities*. But Wild Service is a more radical belief than that: it is about *the right to be responsible*, the right to connect and care. Responsibility derives from response, to be answerable. It is a pledge we make to something with which we are already in a relationship. No relationship, no responsibility. Nothing to answer. Nothing to commit. Nothing to give back.

It is exactly such a culture of responsibility which our history of exclusive land ownership – which still sees half the country owned by 1 per cent of its people – has inhibited, and which the laws of exclusion still frustrate. In its place we have been sold a model of 'stewardship' in which major landowners look after the land on everyone else's behalf. The results, as Guy demonstrates, have been dire: for nature and for ourselves. It is time, as Nick reminds us, that we listened to the wisdom of centuries of collective relationships with the landscape, instead. Nature is calling: we must now all have a share in the answer.

That is why the right to roam is not simply about more room for the exercise of ski poles, or adding to a list of places to go for a swim. Though these things, in their own way, also matter. It is the precondition for an ecological future which cannot emerge so long as we have no widely held relationship with the land.

There are no guarantees here. Changing a law will not, alone, bring that culture about. It is one we will have to build across myriad different facets of our society: from the education of eco-centric beings called for by Emma, to the songdreams we might sing with Sam.

Perhaps we will fail. But we have something powerful on our side. Tune in with Dal to the 'language of vibrations, ripples and waves, wonder and birdsong and dreams, ancestors and ghosts, and gusts of wind' and ask yourself: if this was for everyone, would we really choose anything else?

Wild Service is our manifesto for a grassroots ecology, a paean to the ability of 'ordinary' people to act for nature despite the fences, paywalls and gatekeepers standing in their way. It rejects the unpeopled wilderness fantasies dismantled by Harry's reinterpretation of Muir's Yosemite, holding fast to the belief that diversity of people and the biodiversity of life go hand in hand. And it rejects the arrogance of 'stewardship' with all its implied paternalism and replaces it with the more modest idea of service instead, placing nature above the human, not below.

That modesty is important in other ways. If anyone in this book has asked permission, it has been from the earth itself, not simply those with title to it. But that does not mean rejecting expertise. We must be humble enough to know when we don't know enough, that there is a time to pause and learn, as well as a time to act. We take heed of the lessons learned from the story of the black poplar tree, which allies the finesse of genetic science with the enthusiasm and insight of amateurs, safeguarding the species' diversity while ensuring the scale and impetus to getting its restoration done. Wild Service looks forward to a culture which can push beyond the often private activity documented throughout this book, seeking to translate these pioneering individual acts into a collective culture of care.

We should also acknowledge that the desire, or openness, to change our ecosystems is unevenly distributed. An axiom used by campaigners, drawn from the writing of the writer and activist Adrienne Maree Brown, is that of moving at the pace of trust: focusing on the formation of relationships between people as much as immediate massification of the cause. Here we think of Nicola's immersion in her community, the way she transformed a potentially tricky conversation over lapwing nests into a source of collective pride. It is a principle which perhaps captures the sweet spot between the sometimes over-eager impetus of direct action and the too-slow (or too-corrupt) pace of legislative change. History has left us many justifications for antagonism and, sometimes, few options but antagonism remain. But antagonism alone is a weak shepherd of change. Can we hold in our heads the need to transform society, to transform our ecosystems, to make good on an imbalanced and unjust history, while holding the humanity of those sceptical of such change?

In today's England such questions have other, more specific implications. We firmly invoke Wild Service as a form of participatory belonging which has nothing to do with the arbitrary demarcations of the nation state. But if Wild Service doesn't need England, it feels like England needs Wild Service. Of all the nations on this isle, it suffers most from its vexed relationship with identity. Its imperial history, first subsuming the other countries of the not-so-United Kingdom, before assuming the moniker 'Great Britain' to do the same elsewhere, has left England with a void at its centre: a worrisome sense of what might be left once the pomp of monarchy and the imperial past are peeled away.

Well, the paint is peeling. The walls are looking unstable, the carpets threadbare. And no amount of tabloid screaming about migrants or environmentalists is putting up the book-shelves or steadying the foundations. The thin forms of pseudo-enchantment we have conscripted into our identity crisis — stacking jewels on sceptres and crowns on heads — are looking more desperate than ever.* In its place we need new stories and fresh enchantments, grounded not in the dubious attachments of nationhood or feudal hierarchy, but in the service to nature we undertake together, whoever 'we' are. Wild Service is composed of this 'we', the those-who-turn-up. And, like the church of St Mark's, it always leaves its door ajar.

There is a very English irony here. The prime minister's country house, Chequers, is named after the regional term for the wild service tree, which happens to grow in its grounds. It was gifted to the nation (though, in practice, the state) by the dignitary Arthur Lee, in 1917, to serve as a unifying salve between men of different class and disposition: 'in the city-bred man', Lee hoped, 'the periodic contact with the most typical rural life would create and preserve a just sense of proportion between the claims of town and country.' To the revolutionary statesman 'the antiquity and calm tenacity of Chequers and its annals might suggest some saving virtues in the continuity of English history and exercise a check upon too hasty upheavals, whilst even the most reactionary could scarcely be insensible to the spirit of human freedom which permeates the country-side of Hampden, Burke and Milton'.

The government didn't get the memo. In 2005, Chequers was declared a protected site under the Serious Organised Crime and Police Act, making it one of the few places in the country where trespass is a serious criminal offence. Those wishing to test the spirit of human freedom which permeates its country-side could expect to do up to six months for the pleasure. This

*Apologies to our royalist readers, but can we put 'the rod of equity and mercy' away now?

top-down symbol of national unity, available only to those of rank — if not solely privilege — is one which keeps the door firmly closed. 'The nation' is not enough. Because it is not, in the end, really ours.

In a country broken by environmental decline, political fracture and social division, it is nature, not nation, which provides the most likely source of unification. Because it's real. Because it's meaningful. Because it matters. Because it's dying. And because, without it, we are done. While we can live happily enough in a world without princes, we should refuse to live in one without puffins. Rather than a higher power, let us defer to the lower: the matter of which we are all composed, not illusions we never chose. As Bryony reminds us, the etymology of 'human' is 'humus' — the material into which all our bodies will one day reintegrate, bonding us to 'the same living world that our human systems are currently degrading'. It is to this universal humus we owe our fealty.

It was once the norm in Britain to view ownership as only one of many ways of relating to the land; one which did not necessarily preclude the rights of others to coincident uses or relationships. These common rights represented a parallel 'bundle of rights' to those of property; a kind of counterclaim against ownership being the last, and final, law of the land. Some of those rights, such as estovers (gathering wood) and pannage (the right for your pigs to graze on the forest mast), might seem antiquated today. Some, like digging peat, have been superseded by contemporary ecological concerns. Yet others are still with us. We still, for instance, have the notion of a 'right of way', which allows passage through private property on the basis of historic, customary uses of the land. And though not a right per se, we retain the freedom to forage much of our non-cultivated flora and fungi. Even on private land, what we forage is ours to keep: so long as we uproot no plant, damage no protected species, nor gather for commercial ends.*

A new set of common rights might look different today, building on the baselines of self-sufficiency provided by those in the past to meet new, more incorporeal needs. Some, this book has already begun to outline. Rights of care and healing, the right to belong. Others stretch our concept of what is 'common' altogether, incorporating the rights of nature itself. In places, such meta-rights might be encompassed through more targeted legislation (such as the right to roam, which our campaign has focused on). Or it would redress historic injustices, restoring rights to reside for sustainable or nomadic ways of life, and speak to new means to correct them, such as the community right to buy.

There is room for further top-level, governmental intervention, too. We have floated the idea of a voluntary National Wild Service, replacing the militaristic concept of 'National Service' with opportunities for anyone who wants it to be supported for a year connecting with the land; learning how to exist with it, and making their contribution to the daunting scale of work required to restore it. We might see resources and powers channelled to a more local scale, perhaps a 'Local Environmental Action Fund' (with the pleasing acronym 'LEAF') empowering guardianship groups to intervene when those rights of nature are threatened, acting as nature's advocates and defenders. We can reimagine a

---

*The CRoW Act (2000) introduced a curious anomaly to the law surrounding foraging, making it unlawful to forage on open access land, as new 'rights' supplanted historic freedoms. You consequently have more freedom to forage while trespassing than you do on land to which you have rights of access. Foraging on rights of way remains legitimate, provided you follow the guidelines mentioned and no byelaws prohibit it. Remember, never take the first or the last. Only take what you need in a context of wider abundance. Nature needs its forage, too.

school curriculum which locates our children within the world where they actually live, rather than one which perpetuates their alienation.

It might also prompt the conservation sector to move beyond its traditional role as the gatekeeper of ecological protection towards the empowerment of grassroots ecological change. What would a serious, widespread attempt at massifying nature connection and protection look like if we tried? What would it mean if the role of these organisations was to hand power down, giving people the resources and expertise to hold the agency they have long been denied?

Finally, as the hard boundaries of the land soften, could those who have historically owned it benefit, too? Landowners are often left alone when things go wrong, isolated by their own powers of exclusion from the communities to which they might otherwise belong. When a fly-tip happens or the rhododendron gets out of control, when they want to do the right things by nature but lack the expertise or resources to get them done, could a broader understanding of ownership be an asset, not a divestiture? Like all service, it means giving up a *power over*. It means letting others have a say. But power rarely, in the end, much serves those who hold it. Perhaps Wild Service is the route to a better way.

As I write this epilogue, I take breaks by wandering down the hill to my local river, the Monnow, and clear my head the best way nature has yet invented: by chucking myself into it. To get there, I do the weird rock-climbing move required to circumnavigate the fence the absentee landowner has stuck in the way, and wave at the security cameras they've installed to deter people from coming near. I wander past the signs promising certain death if I continue, and ease myself into the calm waters beyond.

There's something about living with a river. It creeps up on you, one swim to the next, one lazy bankside wander after another. Sink your head through the surface until your eyes hold the balance between sky and water, and you start to see things in ways you can't quite explain. Something about the riotous fizzing of the insects, and the sprat nibbling at your feet. The kingfisher race-tracking over you with its shrill 'cheep'. A river is kind of permanence-in-flux, a question tumbling towards a never-quite-voiced answer.

In the water, my mind drifts downstream where it pours into another river, the Wye, into which the Monnow flows. Over the past decade the Wye has been dying. Saturated by years of phosphate pollution, exacerbated by a surge in giant chicken farms along its rivershed, as well as the chronic dumping of sewage by water companies, it turns a deep soup-green every summer as the supercharged algae takes over, sucking the oxygen from the water and killing the life within. But a fightback is under way. One of the 3 per cent of rivers with a statutory right of navigation, and with near-comprehensive bankside access, the Wye is well known and well loved. It is immortalised in the poetry of Wordsworth and celebrated in the compositions of Elgar. We pay it our homage. As a result, it has one of the most dynamic and active guardianship groups in the country, taking on the politicians, regulators and corporations responsible for its decline, and which have long lied about its neglect.

Correcting such damage will be a long journey. But the polluters are on the back foot, and the condition of the river has been turned into a national scandal. Yet without ordinary people serving as this river's guardians and advocates, we would know little of its fate. They know, because they have been empowered to know: their relationship with the river is enduring.

By contrast, my own river has always had sporadic and fragmented access. After the actions of people like the absentee landowner, it now has even less. A group of anglers do what they can for it. But their numbers alone are not enough and seem to be dwindling (the hobby, overwhelmingly male – and its demographics, ageing). I track the decline of the river's condition in the mournful reports of their annual newsletter and wonder what to do next.

I would soon have my answer. Rivers are natural connectors. And it turned out, the activity on the Wye was having a surprising halo effect, spilling its energy back upstream into its comparatively inaccessible tributaries, where new communities of river protectors were beginning to form in response. It seems fitting that magic should move in the opposite direction to the laws of physics.

I pull myself out of the river, and dry off fast, shivering from the cold of the water. Back at the High Security Zone, the floods have been through and a silty patina is covering the stone slabs on the floor. And that was when I spotted it: a naked footprint, about the same size as my own, tracing its way through the silt ahead, past the security cameras and padlocked gates, the fences and the signs. Somewhere in my small, conservative rural suburb there was another like me. Someone else willing to work through the petty trials of enclosure, and step through the fences as if they were air. I walked home, mind alive with the dream of a fragile possibility. One in which the needs of the river and its excluded neighbours came to supplant the absentee owners of its bank. One in which the gentle motion of feet and hands arrive in community, to affirm forgotten vows in fresh acts of service.

Jon Moses, five minutes uphill of the River Monnow,
July 2023

NOTES

PROLOGUE

1 https://www.countryside-alliance.org/resources/news/over-4-000-crimes-committed-at-churches-in-past-ye

CHAPTER 1

1 Miles Richardson, *Reconnection: Fixing Our Broken Relationship with Nature*, Pelagic Publishing, London, 2023, p. 55.

2 Lucy Jones, *Losing Eden: Why Our Minds Need the Wild*, Penguin Books, London, 2021.

3 Richardson, *Reconnection*, p. 49.

4 Opinium Survey: 5 October 2018.

5 Damian Carrington, 'Three-quarters of UK children spend less time outdoors than prison inmates – survey', *Guardian*, 25 March 2016.

6 C. Clayton and M. Potter, 'New Uses of Screens in Post-Lockdown Britain', University of Leeds, 2022.

7 Miles Richardson, Iain Hamlin, Lewis R. Elliott and Mathew P. White, 'Country-level factors in a failing relationship with nature: Nature connectedness as a key metric for a sustainable future', *Ambio*, 2022.

8 Survey: Office for National Statistics, 'Estimates on relationship with others, volunteering, sense of belonging to a neighbourhood, and say in what the government does for all adults and by age, sex and region, Great Britain: 22 June to 17 July 2022'.

9 Robin Wall Kimmerer, *Braiding Sweetgrass: Indigenous Wisdom, Scientific Knowledge and the Teaching of Plants*, Milkweed Editions, Minneapolis, 2013, p. 208.

10 John Fox, *General View of the Agriculture of the County of Monmouth*, 1794.

11   Charles Hassall, *General View of the Agriculture of the County of Monmouth*, 1815.

12   Ibid.

13   J. M. Neeson, *Commoners: Common Right, Enclosure and Social Change in England 1700–1820*, Cambridge University Press, Cambridge, 1993.

14   Ibid.

15   Peter Brandon, *The Kent and Sussex Weald*, Phillimore & Co., Bognor Regis, 2003, p. 7.

16   Ibid., p. 5.

17   Thomas Rudge, *General View of the Agriculture of the County of Gloucester*, 1807.

18   Charles Vancouver, *General View of the Agriculture of Hampshire, Including the Isle of Wight*, 1810.

19   Rudge, *General View [Gloucester]*.

20   John Clark, *General View of the Agriculture of the County of Hereford* (1794), cited in Neeson, *Commoners*, p. 28.

21   John Clare, 'The Mores', in *Major Works*, Oxford University Press, Oxford, 2008.

22   Clare, 'The Lamentations of Round-Oak Waters', in *Major Works*.

23   Hassall, *General View [Monmouth]*.

24   Rudge, *General View [Gloucester]*.

25   Timothy Nourse, *Campania Foelix, or a Discourse of the Benefits and Improvements of Husbandry*, cited in Neeson, *Commoners*, p. 20.

CHAPTER 2

1   Miles Richardson, *Reconnection: Fixing Our Broken Relationship with Nature*, Pelagic Publishing, London, 2023.

2   https://www.rspb.org.uk/about-the-rspb/about-us/media-centre/press-releases/new-report-shows-the-uk-is-the-least-effective-g7-member-at-protecting-nature/

3   https://www.nationalgeographic.com/environment/article/can-indigenous-land-stewardship-protect-biodiversity-?loggedin=true&rnd=1686917282438

4   Survival International launches campaign to stop '30x30' – 'the biggest land grab in history'

5   https://biol420eres525.wordpress.com/2014/04/06/breaking-out-of-the-fortress-a-biocultural-approach-to-conservation/

CHAPTER 3

1 'Stewardship': *Merriam-Webster Dictionary*, https://www.merriam-webster.com/dictionary/stewardship

2 Genesis 1:26, Bible, King James Version, 1611, https://www.kingjamesbibleonline.org/Genesis-1-26/

3 Lynn White, Jnr, 'The Historical Roots of Our Ecological Crisis', *Science* 155: 1,203–7, 1967, https://www.cmu.ca/faculty/gmatties/lynnwhiterootsofcrisis.pdf

4 Matthew Hale, 'The Great Audit, with the Account of the Good Steward', in *Contemplations Moral and Divine*, 1679 (published posthumously), p. 293.

5 Michael Winter, *Rural Politics: Policies for Agriculture, Forestry and the Environment*, Routledge, 1996, p. 203.

6 CLA press release, 'Education course has potential to shed light on UK food production, says CLA', 21 April 2022, https://www.cla.org.uk/news/education-course-will-shed-light-on-uk-food-production-says-cla/

7 Environment secretary Thérèse Coffey, speech to NFU conference, 22 February 2023, https://www.gov.uk/government/speeches/secretary-of-state-therese-coffey-addresses-nfu-conference

8 Farmland bird populations declined by 58% between 1970 and 2020. See DEFRA National Statistics, 'Wild Bird Populations in the UK, 1970 to 2021', updated 13 April 2023, https://www.gov.uk/government/statistics/wild-bird-populations-in-the-uk/wild-bird-populations-in-the-uk-1970-to-2021#breeding-farmland-bird-populations-in-the-uka-name--2-breeding-farmland-bird-populations-in-the-uka

9 Natural History Museum, 'Britain's rural hedgehogs see dramatic population decline', 22 February 2022, https://www.nhm.ac.uk/discover/news/2022/february/britains-rural-hedgehogs-see-dramatic-population-decline.html; Buglife, 'Bugs Matter survey finds that UK flying insects have declined by nearly 60% in less than 20 years', 5 May 2022, https://www.buglife.org.uk/news/bugs-matter-survey-finds-that-uk-flying-insects-have-declined-by-nearly-60-in-less-than-20-years/

10 What the Science Says (website run by the Game and Wildlife Conservation Trust, GWCT), 'Estimating the number and biomass of pheasants in Britain', 14 July 2020, https://www.whatthesciences

ays.org/estimating-the-number-and-biomass-of-pheasants-in-brit
ain/; Lucy R. Mason et al., RSPB Research Report No. 66, 'The
impacts of non-native gamebird release in the UK: an updated
evidence review', October 2020, https://www.rspb.org.uk/globa
lassets/mason-et-al-2020-rspb-gamebird-review-1-compressed.pdf

11 S. Stroud, M. Fennell, J. Mitchley, S. Lydon, J. Peacock and K. L.
Bacon, 'The botanical education extinction and the fall of plant
awareness', *Ecology and Evolution*, 12, 2022, e9019, https://doi.
org/10.1002/ece3.9019

12 Alex Morrs, ' "Not just weeds": how rebel botanists are
using graffiti to name forgotten flora', *Guardian*, 1 May 2020,
https://www.theguardian.com/environment/2020/may/01/
not-just-weeds-how-rebel-botanists-are-using-graffiti-to-name-
forgotten-flora-aoe. See also the More Than Weeds website founded
by Sophie Leguil, https://morethanweeds.co.uk/

13 Jonathan Morris, ' "Rebel botanists" in Plymouth identify urban
plants', BBC News Devon, 8 September 2020, https://www.bbc.
co.uk/news/av/uk-england-devon-54012372

14 Greenpeace website, 'How Greenpeace creates change': 'These
principles are inspired by the Quaker concept of "bearing witness",
which is about taking action based on conscience … When taking
physical action to stop an environmental wrong isn't possible,
"bearing witness" through one's physical presence at the scene of
the crime is another way to act on conscience and remind those
responsible that they have a higher responsibility than the corporate
bottom line.' https://www.greenpeace.org.uk/about-greenpeace/
how-we-create-change/

15 Moorland Monitors website frontpage, https://moorlandmonit
ors.org/

16 See, for example: Wild Moors press release, 'Shocking new statistics
show over 1,200 fires set in England's nature sites by grouse moors',
30 May 2022, https://www.wildmoors.org.uk/shocking-new-sta
tistics-show-over-1200-fires-set-in-englands-nature-sites-by-gro
use-moors/. On 10 May 2023, Midhope Moor in the Peak District
was the first estate to be successfully prosecuted for breach of the
Heather and Grass Burning Regulations, as a result of evidence
provided by RSPB and other volunteer moorland monitors. See
RSPB website, 'RSPB welcomes progress on moorland burning', 11

May 2023, https://group.rspb.org.uk/sheffield/news-blogs/news/good-news-on-moorland-burning/

17 Moorland Monitors website, 'Heather burning', https://moorland monitors.org/heather-burning/

CHAPTER 4

1 Craig M. Kauffman and Pamela L. Martin, *The Politics of Rights of Nature: Strategies for Building a More Sustainable Future*, MIT Press, Cambridge, MA, 2021.

2 Te Awa Tupua (Whanganui River Claims Settlement) Act 2017.

CHAPTER 5

1 Muir: https://www.smithsonianmag.com/history/john-muirs-yosemite-10737/

2 George: https://www.tulalipnews.com/wp/2014/07/05/american-indians-share-their-yosemite-story/

3 Kroeber: https://www.yosemite.ca.us/library/kroeber/miwok.html

4 Woodburn: https://files.libcom.org/files/EGALITARIAN%20SOCIETIES%20-%20James%20Woodburn.pdf

5 M. D. Spence, *Dispossessing the Wilderness: Indian Removal and the Making of the National Parks*, Oxford University Press, Cary, NC, 1999, p. 119.

6 Muir: https://vault.sierraclub.org/john_muir_exhibit/writings/the_mountains_of_california/chapter_5.aspx

7 Ibid.

8 NPS: https://www.nps.gov/yose/learn/management/statistics.htm

9 Scholl and Taylor: https://pubmed.ncbi.nlm.nih.gov/20405793/

10 George: https://www.fresnobee.com/news/special-reports/yosemite-at-150/article19521750.html

11 George: https://www.tulalipnews.com/wp/2014/07/05/american-indians-share-their-yosemite-story/

12 Banerjee and Arjaliès: https://journals.sagepub.com/doi/pdf/10.1177/26317877211036714

13 Dowie: https://www.theguardian.com/environment/2009/jun/03/yosemite-conservation-indigenous-people

14 Survival International: https://survivalinternational.org/tribes/jenu-kuruba

15 Survival International: https://survivalinternational.org/tribes/bakamessokdja

16 Standing Bear: https://www.huffpost.com/entry/wilderness-preservation_b_942220

17 Mongabay: https://news.mongabay.com/2017/03/new-research-shows-role-ancient-peoples-might-have-played-in-shaping-amazon-rainforest/

18 UNFCCC: https://unfccc.int/news/how-indigenous-peoples-enrich-climate-action

19 Berger: https://mondediplo.com/2006/02/18berger

20 https://www.survivalinternational.org/tribes/yanomami

21 Kopenawa Yanomami, 'The Falling Sky: Words of a Yanomami Shaman', https://www.jstor.org/stable/j.ctt6wppk9

22 *Independent*, https://www.independent.co.uk/climate-change/news/wildflower-meadows-farms-agriculture-flowers-environment-brexit-butterflies-bees-defra-a8433541.html

23 Kimmerer: https://oregonhumanities.org/rll/podcast/episode/democracy-of-species/

THE ARCHITECTURE OF BELONGING: CAIRN

1   https://www.newyorker.com/culture/rabbit-holes/people-are-stacking-too-many-stones

CHAPTER 8

1   https://tradfolk.co/art/art-interviews/weven-shop/

2   https://www.thelostwords.org/spell-songs-history/

3   https://lithub.com/the-wyrd-ones-a-conversation-between-robert-macfarlane-and-johnny-flynn/

4   https://www.theguardian.com/uk-news/2022/apr/20/fears-over-right-to-roam-in-england-as-ministers-wind-up-review

5   https://www.dailymail.co.uk/news/article-10140433/Dont-risk-swimming-Britains-rivers-says-Environment-Agency-boss.html#:~:text=And%20Mr%20Leyland%20replied%3A%20%27The,fish%20that%20live%20within%20them.

6   https://www.aboriginal-art-australia.com/aboriginal-art-library/aboriginal-dreamtime/

WILD SERVICE IN ACTION: LIZ AND THE REBEL BOTANISTS

1   www.rebelbotanists.org
2   The French botanist Boris Presseq pioneered this idea in France, see https://www.boudulemag.com/2019/05/jungle-urbaine. See also Alex Morris, ' "Not just weeds": how rebel botanists are using graffiti to name forgotten flora', *Guardian*, 1 May 2020, https://www.theguardian.com/environment/2020/may/01/not-just-weeds-how-rebel-botanists-are-using-graffiti-to-name-forgotten-flora-aoe
3   Helena Horton, 'Half of Britain and Ireland's native plants have declined over 20 years – study', *Guardian*, 8 March 2023, https://www.theguardian.com/environment/2023/mar/08/half-of-britain-and-irelands-native-plants-have-declined-over-20-years-study
4   Sandra Laville, ' "A disgrace": more than 100 trees cut down in Plymouth despite local opposition', *Guardian*, 15 March 2023, https://www.theguardian.com/environment/2023/mar/15/a-disgrace-more-than-100-trees-cut-down-in-plymouth-despite-local-opposition
5   Tweet by Martyn Oates, Political Editor at BBC South West, 5 May 2023, https://twitter.com/bbcmartynoates/status/1654309632980967424

CHAPTER 10

1   Robin Wall Kimmerer, ' "Ki" to signify a being of the living earth. Not "he" or "she," but "ki." So that when we speak of Sugar Maple, we say, "Oh, that beautiful tree, ki is giving us sap again this spring." And we'll need a plural pronoun, too, for those Earth beings. Let's make that new pronoun "kin".' https://theecologist.org/2015/apr/25/living-beings-our-kith-and-kin-we-need-new-pronoun-nature
2   Saidiya Hartman, from the introduction, 'A Note on Method', to her book *Wayward Lives, Beautiful Experiments*, W. W. Norton, New York, 2020.
3   Estimates vary from 75,000 women to over 100,000 women depending on sources. It's impossible to estimate exact figures. Many women denied they had been raped to avoid damaging family honour or being cast out. In *The Great Partition*, Yale University Press, London, 2017, Yasmin Khan describes, 'Children watched

as their parents were dismembered or burned alive, women were brutally raped and had their breasts and genitals mutilated and entire populations of villages were summarily executed' (p. 129).

4   Throughout this period many women ended their lives by suicide as an alternative to violence, rape, forced pregnancy, loss of honour. On 15 March 1947 in Thoa Khalsa, near Rawalpindi, while their village was being attacked, an estimated ninety women jumped into a well and drowned. While some may have made their own choices to do this, there is no doubt some would've been coerced. 'As Urvashi Butalia remarked, the lines between choice and coercion must have been blurred. Seven decades have passed since the partition, it is almost impossible to find the truth about what exactly happened there' (2022), https://www.hinducollegegazette.com/post/partition-and-patriarchy-the-story-of-thoa-khalsa

5   https://www.goodreads.com/quotes/569473-if-you-are-doing-the-right-thing-for-the-earth

6   brontë velez's question to Tricia Hersey, The Nap Bishop, 'How will you be useless to capitalism today?' (2021), https://thenapministry.wordpress.com/2021/08/03/how-will-you-be-useless-to-capitalism-today/

7   Inspired by the political pamphlet and manifesto 'Revolutionary Ecology' by Peaks of Colour. The seeds of this manifesto were planted during a manifesto-building walkshop I co-facilitated in June 2022 in the Peak District, with self-identifying women and gender diverse POC. Evie Muir describes this as '… a co-curated manifesto that proudly demands racial, gendered and land justice. Ecology is defined as the relationships between people and their environments. It comes from the Greek word for home. Here, we offer you our Revolutionary Ecology: our Home for Revolution.'

8   https://www.iisd.org/articles/deep-dive/indigenous-peoples-defending-environment-all#:~:text=There%20are%20approximately%20370%20million,effective%20stewards%20of%20the%20environment.

EPILOGUE

1   Richard Mabey, *Flora Britannica*: entry for 'Wild Service Tree', Chatto & Windus, London, 1996, p. 204.

2   Ibid.

Jon Moses

Jon Moses is a writer and co-director of the Right to Roam campaign. He has a PhD in Geohumanities from the University of London and has written essays, profiles and reportage for a range of publications including the *Guardian, Businessweek* and *The Lead*. He is currently learning to track animals and shares their antipathy for fences.

Nadia Shaikh

Nadia Shaikh is a naturalist and ornithologist. She is co-director of the Right to Roam campaign and has set up the Raven Network, a group for people of colour working in the environmental and conservation sector, and is working to decolonise the way we think about saving nature. She is a trustee for the Wildlife and Countryside Link and has previously worked for the RSPB and Staffordshire Wildlife Trust. She lives on the Isle of Bute where she has the right to roam. She is learning how to install woodburners and is trying to write a book, but gets distracted by rockpooling.

Guy Shrubsole

Guy Shrubsole is an environmental campaigner and author of *The Lost Rainforests of Britain* (William Collins, 2022) and *Who Owns England?* (William Collins, 2019). He co-founded the Right to Roam campaign, and has previously worked for Rewilding Britain, Friends of the Earth and the Department for the Environment, Food and Rural Affairs (DEFRA). He lives in Devon.

Paul Powlesland

Paul Powlesland is a barrister and founder of Lawyers for Nature, which aims to transform the relationship between law, lawyers and the natural world. He acts to protect trees and rivers in the courts and campaigns for the Rights of Nature. He lives on a boat on the River Roding in East London, and set up the River Roding Trust to protect and restore the river.

Harry Jenkinson

Harry Jenkinson is a land justice and Indigenous rights campaigner. He has conducted ethnographic research on indigenous ecological perspectives in Papua New Guinea and Greenland. In 2021 he co-founded Landscapes of Freedom, an organisation dedicated to supporting access to nature throughout Sussex. He joined the Right to Roam campaign in 2022. In his spare time, he enjoys regular walks in nature and imagining utopian futures.

Amy-Jane Beer

Amy-Jane Beer is a biologist by training, a writer by practice, but probably a witch by nature. Since earning a doctorate in the metamorphoses of sea urchins, she underwent a few developmental transformations of her own, from researcher to editor to science writer, conservationist, naturalist and campaigner — a multidisciplinary career path which informs her thinking and writing. Her recent book, *The Flow: Rivers, Water and Wildness* (Bloomsbury Wildlife, 2023), won the James Cropper Wainwright Prize for nature writing in 2023. She is a long-serving Country Diarist for the *Guardian* and columnist for *British Wildlife* magazine. She lives in North Yorkshire, witnessing the best and worst of landownership and management practices on her doorstep.

Nicola Chester

Nicola Chester has been an activist for nature, particularly in our rural landscape, for many years, even before her involvement in the road protests of the 1990s. She writes columns for the *RSPB* and *Countryfile* magazines and is a *Guardian* Country Diarist. Her memoir, *On Gallows Down* (Chelsea Green Publishing, 2021), won the Richard Jefferies Award and was Highly Commended for the James Cropper Wainwright Prize, 2022. She has worked with horses, the Conservation Volunteers, been a cowgirl and is now a secondary school librarian – while always writing in defence of nature. A long-term tenant in a former tied cottage in the North Wessex Downs, she and her husband have raised three children. She has witnessed the local extinctions of far too many birds, insects and wildflowers, but believes in hope, predicated by action and connection. www.nicolachester.wordpress.com @nicolawriting

Nick Hayes

Nick Hayes is a co-founder of the Right to Roam campaign and author of *The Trespasser's Companion*, *The Book of Trespass* and four graphic novels. Winner of two World Illustration awards, he makes his living through illustration, and loses it again through campaigning. He is currently working with high-profile manufacturers to design a mass producible 3D-printed guillotine, to save us all some time.

Sam Lee

Folksinger, song collector, activist, nature conservationist, guide and presenter, Sam Lee has spent eighteen years re-galvanising the sight, sound and ecosystem of the folk arts in the UK through his projects and live shows. With three critically acclaimed albums, his debut receiving a Mercury Music Prize nomination, Sam works holistically in challenging the very nature of our indigenous music in the twenty-first century. Sam is the producer and lead artist in many projects marrying nature, music and community. Most notably, in 2019 he got birdsong to No. 18 in the UK singles charts with the RSPB and he's the creator of the sellout Singing With Nightingales series, which gave rise to his debut book *The Nightingale* (Penguin, 2021). Sam has worked extensively with the environmental sector to lead campaigns and projects highlighting the climate and ecological crisis globally as well as at home. His practice focuses on finding ways of leading people into a deeper more sensitive connection to nature and communicating the treasures on our own doorsteps through song and storytelling as well as immersive experiences, pilgrimages and nature guiding. www.samlee s ong.co.uk @samleesong

Emma Linford

Emma Linford is a campaigner, expedition guide and educator whose advocacy intersects regenerative education, social activism and land justice. Her leadership is grounded in twenty years of facilitating transformative experiences for over 5,000 humans from diverse social backgrounds on multi-day journeys worldwide, from the UK National Parks to the Canadian Arctic. She is intent on bringing the other-than-human into these politics as a necessary opportunity to change toxic popular culture and enable future generations to have better relationships to self, community and local and planetary landscapes. She co-leads the Stars are for Everyone campaign, lectures at Schumacher College, is a member of the British Association of International

Mountain Leaders, an RGS fellow and an accredited practitioner for the Institute of Outdoor Learning.

Dal Kular

Dal Kular is a writer and facilitator of creative and nature-allied writing arts for healing, liberation and joy. She left school at sixteen with three O-levels having been told she could never be a writer – returning to the power of words in her late forties as an act of radical care and healing. Her debut poetry book *(un) interrupted tongues* is published by Fly on the Wall Press. Dal was shortlisted for the Queen Mary Wasafiri New Writing Prize and the Class Action Nature Writing Prize in 2021 and was a recipient of an Arts Council England Developing Your Creative Practice Grant. She loves making zines and botanical journals, is an allotment keeper and loves roaming the Peak District in her tiny campervan. She's currently working on an archival justice commission with Dig Where You Stand, Sheffield, and is Peaks of Colour 2024 Writer-in-Residence. She lives in Sheffield. www.dalkular.com; https://dalkular.substack.com

Bryony Ella

Bryony Ella paints in the studio, draws in the wild and creates public art installations in the city. Her practice explores human–nature relationships at the intersection of science and spirituality, often through collaboration with activists, academics and organisations such as the British Council, Butterfly Conservation, the UK Centre for Ecology and Hydrology and the Grantham Research Institute on Climate Change and the Environment. Currently, she is living and working between London and New York, where she is employed as Research Artist on an environmental history project exploring sensory experiences of urban heat. https://

www.studiobryonyella.com/; Instagram: @studiobryonyella;
Substack: @embodiedecology

Romilly Swann

Romilly Swann is a shepherdess and natural dyer living by
the Thames in Oxfordshire. With a background in botany and
archaeology she is currently twining her roles as an illustrator,
educator and writer to question and explore human nature, nostalgia and relationships with the land and natural world within a
swiftly evolving countryside.

Maria Fernandez Garcia

Maria Fernandez Garcia is an educator and founder of Healing
Weeds, a space to learn about wild food and medicine. Maria has
been an outdoors educator for over five years, and is a champion
of using modern scientific research to support traditional uses of
medicinal wild plants. Maria joined the campaign in early 2023
to support Right to Roam local groups as they reclaim their relationship to the land around them.

A NOTE ON THE AUTHOR

Nick Hayes is an author, illustrator, print-maker and political cartoonist. He has published four graphic novels with Jonathan Cape and has worked for, among others, the *Literary Review*, *Time Out*, the British Council, the and the *Guardian*. He has exhibited across the country, including at the Hayward Gallery. He lives on a canal-boat with no fixed address.

A NOTE ON THE TYPE

The text of this book is set in Fournier. Fournier is derived from the romain du roi, which was created towards the end of the seventeenth century from eight designs made by a committee of the Académie of Sciences for the exclusive use of the Imprimerie Royale. The original Fournier types were cut by the famous Paris founder Pierre Simon Fournier in about 1742. These types were some of the most influential designs of the eight and are counted among the earliest examples of the 'transitional' style of typeface. This Monotype version dates from 1924. Fournier is a light, clear face whose distinctive features are capital letters that are quite tall and bold in relation to the lower-case letters, and *decorative italics, which show the influence of the calligraphy of Fournier's time.*